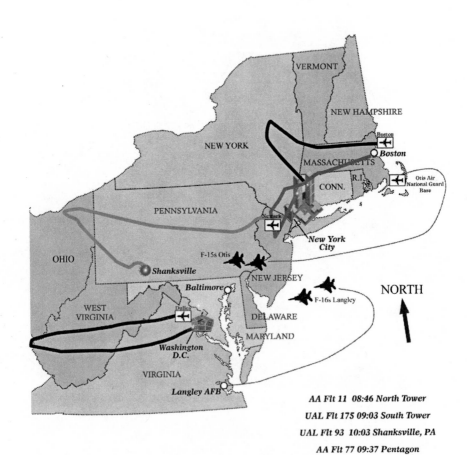

AA Flt 11 08:46 North Tower
UAL Flt 175 09:03 South Tower
UAL Flt 93 10:03 Shanksville, PA
AA Flt 77 09:37 Pentagon

9/11/01 Aircraft Routes of Flight

24 Hours Inside
the President's Bunker

9-11-01
The White House

A PERSONAL ACCOUNT OF
THE UNPRECEDENTED ACTIONS TAKEN
TO DEFEND AMERICA

Robert J. Darling
Lieutenant Colonel, USMC (Ret.)

Foreword by Reverend Andrew J. Heintz

iUniverse, Inc.
New York   Bloomington

24 Hours inside the President's Bunker
9-11-01: The White House

The views expressed in this work are solely those of the author and do not necessarily reflect the views of the publisher, and the publisher hereby disclaims any responsibility for them.

iUniverse books may be ordered through booksellers or by contacting:

iUniverse
1663 Liberty Drive
Bloomington, IN 47403
www.iuniverse.com
1-800-Authors (1-800-288-4677)

Because of the dynamic nature of the Internet, any Web addresses or links contained in this book may have changed since publication and may no longer be valid.

ISBN: 978-1-4502-4423-7 (sc)
ISBN: 978-1-4502-4424-4 (dj)
ISBN: 978-1-4502-4425-1 (ebk)

Library of Congress Control Number: 2010909863

Printed in the United States of America

iUniverse rev. date: 7/29/2010

The National Security Council has reviewed the contents of this book for the purpose of safeguarding our country's classified information and has approved it for publication.

Si vis pacem, para bellum
(If you wish for peace, prepare for war!)

—*Publius Flavius Vegetius Renatus*

For my wife, Angela, who simply inspires me on so many levels, and my two sons Michael and Matthew, for the joy they bring, the humility they inflict, and the incredible love we all share for each other.

And for my parents, for all you've given me—especially the courage to try new things, the strength to overcome adversity, and the character to make real friends along the way; I love you both.

CONTENTS

Acknowledgments xiii

Foreword xv

Introduction xix

Prologue xxiii

Chapter 1   North of Manhattan 1

Chapter 2   The Call of the Corps 5

Chapter 3   My Road to the White House 15

Chapter 4   White House Duty 31

Chapter 5   A Morning Unlike Any Other 37

Chapter 6   The Attack 43

Chapter 7   The PEOC 49

Chapter 8   The Aftermath: September 12, 2001 91

Chapter 9   Angela's Story 95

Chapter 10 Conclusion 101

Afterword 103

Glossary of Terms 127

About the Author 139

Index 141

ACKNOWLEDGMENTS

When I began the task of writing this book, I had no idea how many people would eventually contribute their time, talents, and patience into making this a reality. I am truly grateful to all of you.

I would like to first thank God for the many blessings in my life, including my truly wonderful family, the good health we enjoy, and the opportunity to serve this great nation as a United States Marine. I want to thank my father-in-law, Dr. Eduardo Paderon, for convincing me that I not only had the ability to write this important piece of American history, but the responsibility to do it as well.

I would also like to thank my friends, especially Father Andrew Heintz, for his prayers, editorial talent, tenacity, and very candid advice. His contributions to this effort were immeasurable. Amy Fowler took on the tough task of helping me "organize and set the stage." Col. Tom Sharpy, John Harrison, Michael McMahon, Col. Scott Whitaker, Sarah Moyer, and Stu Paul for their skill, enthusiasm, expertise, and support. Linda Cashdan and Jim Moor, I couldn't have done this without you. I thank Major Richard T. Spooner, USMC (Ret.), for introducing me to his friends and becoming one of mine. I also offer a sincere thanks to Secretary Prinsipi and FBI Agent John for providing the interviews for this book and for all they've done and continue to do for our country.

In addition, I would also like to thank New York City Firefighter Mark Heintz and his brother firemen from Engine 167 & Ladder 87 in Staten Island, and the firemen of "10 House" in lower Manhattan. Thanks for making me feel welcome and for listening to my 9/11 story and for sharing yours. It was an honor to get to know you. You are indeed New York's bravest.

To my wife, Angela: thank you for your love, encouragement, and support.

And lastly, I truly want to thank our nation's military and first responders; you have endured the hardship of multiple deployments, faced our enemies in combat, defended our homeland, protected our freedoms, and thwarted all of their attempts to bring terror to our cities and into our homes. You have risen to the challenge of our time and answered the call of our nation. You are our heroes.

FOREWORD

24 Hours Inside the President's Bunker is the story of Marine Corps Lt. Col. Robert Darling and his account of what took place at the top of the United States chain of command on September 11, 2001, as the U.S. government struggled to respond to the sudden terrorist strike launched against our nation. Lt. Col. Darling offers us a bird's-eye view of the dramatic events that unfolded above and beneath the White House grounds in the minutes and hours after the first strikes occurred. As a military liaison officer to the president, Lt. Col. Darling was on hand to coordinate presidential airlift assets, but was quickly tasked to directly assist the presidential response team, which was hurriedly assembled in the White House bunker. As the story unfolds, one is left riveted by the fast-paced action and the response of Vice President Cheney and others who were forced to make dramatic and historic decisions at a lightning pace, potentially affecting millions of people—and to do so with little or no deliberation.

The purpose of the book is to provide an accurate and concise historical account of the crisis decision making that took place at the White House during the twenty-four hours surrounding the 9/11 attacks on our country. As such, the book offers an invaluable contribution to scholars, historians, political and military leaders, intelligence officers, students of crisis diplomacy, and the average citizen who is concerned with how our government responds to crisis. The book offers us a unique view of our national effort to defend our country and quickly communicate with concerned leaders around the world. Lt. Col. Darling provides an honest and clear assessment of various successes and failures that took place in the presidential chain of command, starting with the National Command Authority and extending down to local military, government, and civilian leaders. As in any crisis, not everything went as planned, and both the strengths and weaknesses in the U.S. command and control structure were revealed.

With careful attention to detail, Lt. Col. Darling paints for us a complete picture of the command, control, and communication response to the most dramatic attack on our nation since Pearl Harbor. As one reads, one can see the crisis unfold not just on one but on three levels of decision making. One level is between the air-traffic controllers and the various airlines involved in the hijackings; another level is between the air-traffic controllers and the military and FAA officials called in to help them respond to the hijackings; and the third level is between the National Command Authority and the FAA and the military. To add to the complexity, one can see how events begin to unfold across several sectors of airspace and eventually include the entire Northeastern region of the United States. Not even the official 9/11 Commission Report offers us such a complete and personal account of what really happened underground at the White House on that most fateful day.

Lt. Col. Darling also offers the reader a brief account of his own life, which is in itself inspiring. Like many of his fellow Marines, Bob is a great patriot, a loyal friend, and a fine American. Bob was raised in upstate New York, went to Iona College, and joined the Marine Corps at an early age. I firmly believe that, as Americans, we owe Bob and his fellow Marines a tremendous debt of gratitude for their service to our nation, both in peace and at war. He is part of that 1 percent who has served to defend the other 99 percent of us, who are sitting safely at home or at work when the fighting occurs.

It is hard to believe that after nine long years, the war on terror continues to rage. Given the clear and ongoing threat from Islamic radicals, we no doubt will find ourselves in the same or similar circumstances in the near future. We need to remain ever vigilant in the face of constant attempts to attack us from all different angles. As Lt. Col. Darling's book exposes, our government tends to react very slowly and bureaucratically, even in dire emergencies. This book is a clarion call to properly organize and equip our national leaders, on all levels, to respond as quickly and efficiently as possible to any such future crisis. And though he recognizes that efforts have been made to streamline decision making and response time, Lt. Col. Darling also points out that more needs to be done. The White House and top Pentagon brass need to closely examine the activities of the National Command Authority on 9/11 and implement some serious measures to bridge the leadership gaps that occurred on account of both technical and human failure.

This book is long overdue. What started as a lecture given in various venues and circumstances—including as part of a 9/11 memorial lecture series delivered in several of the parishes in which I have served—Lt. Col. Darling's 9/11 story has now been elevated to a book of national import.

May God, our Eternal Father, grant wisdom and strength to all of those called to protect and defend our great nation, and may God bless us and remain with us at all times, but especially in moments of difficulty or need.

Reverend Father Andrew J. Heintz, Diocese of Arlington, VA
MA (International Relations), M.Div., MA (Theology)
Alexandria, Virginia

INTRODUCTION

On September 11, 2001, nineteen al-Qaeda terrorists hijacked four commercial airliners, crashing two of the airliners into the Twin Towers of the World Trade Center in New York; a third into the Pentagon near Washington DC; and the fourth plane into a field near Shanksville, Pennsylvania.

2,976 innocent lives were lost,
and our world was changed forever.

And yet, despite the terrorists' best efforts, they ultimately failed in their attempt to decapitate our government, cripple our financial system, and drive us into a state of fear and isolation. Rather than destroy us, their actions unified us. Immediately following the 9/11 attacks, we put our political affiliations and personal divides aside and came together as one nation, indivisible, as other freedom-loving nations from around the world joined us in our global fight to defeat radical Islamic extremists and the rogue regimes that harbored them. I will always cherish the memories of the flag-draped neighborhoods, the cheering crowds supporting our first responders at Ground Zero, the chills I felt hearing all fifty thousand spectators at a professional sporting event singing our national anthem with pride and purpose, and the overwhelming sense of patriotism I felt when strangers walked up to me on the street to say, "Thanks for your service to our country."

No one will ever forget where they were or who they were with at that precise moment in time when they either turned on their televisions and saw those unimaginable images, looked out their windows at the sky filled with billowing smoke, or felt the foundations of the buildings they were in shake under their feet. For most of us, however, our 9/11 memories begin at that moment when we received that frantic call from a friend or loved one shouting, "Turn on the TV—our country is under attack!" It's an event that has been seared in our minds forever.

This is my 9/11 story.

It begins with my journey to become a Marine Corps officer and an attack helicopter pilot serving in Desert Shield, Desert Storm, and in Somalia. It continues through my time flying as a pilot for the President of the United States and eventually working as an Airlift Operations officer for the White House Military Office.

On 9/11, as the attack on America was in progress, I responded to the underground White House bunker known as the President's Emergency Operations Center, or PEOC. From there, I directly supported Vice President Dick Cheney and the National Security Advisor, Dr. Condoleezza Rice, with real-time, unfiltered information being passed to us from the White House Situation Room and the Pentagon. I witnessed firsthand the enormity of the crisis leadership decisions that were made that day on behalf of all Americans as our enemies tried to bring America to her knees. As a result of our enemy's actions and those critical decisions made to defend her, we are now a nation at war, conceivably for a generation to come.

In the afterword, I reflect back on what was perceived to be a complete failure of the National Command Authority, the governing body made up of the President of the United States and the Secretary of Defense. Since the Cold War, the NCA has been the ultimate, lawful authority over the actions of the United States military. On 9/11, the President was faced with technological problems on board Air Force One and could not communicate well with his top advisors in the White House. He and the Vice President were repeatedly cut off from one another throughout the course of the day. The Secretary of Defense, however, never even attempted to contact the President during the one-hour-and-seventeen-minute attack on our nation. By his own admission to the 9/11 Commission, he did not speak to the President or issue any orders to the military to defend America until well after the attack had ended. Had it not been for the decisive actions of Vice President Cheney to insert himself into the military chain of command and order the Pentagon to take action, there would have been no *official* response to the attacks from the entire executive branch of our government.

One may also notice in certain places throughout this book that the timeline of events, as I present them, differs significantly from those listed in the news media and in the 9/11 Commission Report. The fact is that I, along with other key members of the White House Military Office, who served in significant capacities in the PEOC that day, were never consulted or asked to provide our notes to anyone. Nor were we ever contacted by any member of the 9/11 Commission for an interview.

To help you with the military terms, acronyms, and agencies, I've included a glossary in the back of the book.

PROLOGUE

On June 6, 1987, from the gleaming deck of the USS *Intrepid*, a floating military museum moored in the Hudson River, with the Manhattan skyline behind me, I raised my right hand and swore a time-honored oath to protect and defend the Constitution of the United States against all enemies, foreign and domestic. With that pledge, affirmed in God's name, I received my military commission and became Second Lieutenant Robert Joseph Darling, United States Marine Corps. In the distance, the Twin Towers of the World Trade Center stood like a pair of Marines at brace: tall, resolute, indestructible. As my mom, Jeanette Darling, and my godmother, Maureen Morris, affixed the single gold bars to my uniform, I knew that my life had finally taken a path toward something meaningful—a path that was not my parents', not my brothers', not something I was told to do. It was mine and mine alone.

Over the next fourteen years, my experiences as a Marine aviator would prepare me for a day of decision making and action unlike any other I would face in my lifetime.

CHAPTER 1

NORTH OF MANHATTAN

Growing up in Newburgh, New York, in the late 1970s and early 1980s as the third of four sons, I knew deep down that the role model my father, Michael Darling, presented as a dedicated police officer, hardworking business owner, and entrepreneur, while honorable, was not exactly the model I saw for myself. My oldest brother, Sean, was by far the hardest working and most studious of all of us—very dependable. There was no question in anyone's mind that he would grow up and do well for himself. Denis was second in line to the Darling family throne. He had the highest IQ out of the bunch and could fix anything. Problem was, he was usually the one who had broken it to begin with. (I was born just a short ten and a half months behind him; we'll get to me soon enough.) Finally, there was my brother Neil. As the youngest of four boys, he grew up to be both smart and tough. As kids, Neil and Denis were regular sparring partners; despite the five-year gap in their ages, they usually fought to a draw. Sean was to be the family lawyer, Denis the engineer, and Neil the bouncer or professional football player.

Although I didn't know precisely what it was I wanted to be, or the trajectory I wanted my life to follow, I did know, all too well, that I was hardly an A student. When asked the ubiquitous question always posed by well-meaning family and friends, "What do you want to do when you grow up, Bob?" I was invariably vague in my response or just preferred to avoid the question altogether. During one such parental counseling session, I distinctly remember my parents voicing their concern over my apparent apathy and general lack of focus or enthusiasm for anything in particular by asking, "Bob, if today were 'pick your career' day at school, what is it you'd choose to be?" My response was usually something along the lines of, "Ahh, nothing, I guess," or "I haven't decided yet." And then there was the "any number of things" response designed to simply deflect the question altogether. I would overhear my frustrated dad voice his concern to my mom by commenting, "That kid is so unambitious that if the chain on his bicycle ever fell off, it would be broken forever."

Learning how to fix something or to figure out how things worked was not my forte; I was the kind of guy whose VCR would flash 12:00 forever, and I'd be just fine with that. But even as I wondered about my future, I drove myself hard on the ice whenever a game of hockey presented itself. It was my one true passion, and it consumed me. My desire to excel on skates enabled me to become a standout player during both my high-school years and as a freshman walk-on player on the Iona College hockey team. I was strong and fast, but I just didn't get as much ice time as I would have liked—just a few minutes per game at times—and I wanted more. As my college years passed, I realized that despite my love of the game, it was apparent that I just didn't have the required talent to make a living playing it.

Choosing to attend Iona College in New Rochelle, New York, had been a great decision. I knew right off that it was the perfect setting for me. The small, private college, run by Iona's Christian Brothers, helped me grow and mature into a young man looking for his niche in life. The one-on-one attention I received from my professors, the camaraderie of my fellow hockey players, and the proximity to Manhattan made my years at Iona truly the best four years of my young-adult life.

Nonetheless, I was anxious about what waited for me beyond college. I struggled to target a post-college profession while, to my increasing unease, most of my buddies seemed to know exactly what they were going to do. Whether they involved graduate school, a corporate management training program, or teaching, their plans went on and on. Even though I wasn't sure what my future held, I knew I liked business, and I knew I liked money. Growing up on the outskirts of the nation's financial center, I figured if there was anything I thought I could be, it was a stockbroker, and so I focused on economics; that became my goal. But, as I entered my junior year, a whole new career dimension unexpectedly opened up right in front of me.

CHAPTER 2

THE CALL OF THE CORPS

One day in early October of 1985, as I was walking across campus, I saw two friends, Tim Sullivan and John McGyver, and couldn't help but notice that their appearances had undergone dramatic transformations over the summer break, to say the very least. Quite frankly, I couldn't believe it. Their heads were closely shaved, and they looked as if they were in better-than-great shape. Somehow, they seemed taller, more confident, and I couldn't help but notice the crisp gait to their walk, rather than the usual slouching saunter seen everywhere on campus. I remember running over to them and asking, "Hey, what happened to you guys?"

McGyver and Sullivan told me they'd spent the summer at Quantico, Virginia, at the Marine Corps' Platoon Leader Class (PLC), an alternative to the Naval Reserve Officer Training Course (NROTC) for college students wanting to become officers in the Marine Corps. Students can enroll in PLC when they are freshmen, sophomores, or juniors. For freshmen or sophomores, enrollment means attending two six-week summer training programs at the Marine Corps Officer Candidate School (OCS) at Quantico, while students who enroll in the program as juniors attend one ten-week summer course.

The PLC class sizes are typically two hundred fifty to three hundred students, broken up into four to six platoons. The platoons train in both a physically and emotionally demanding environment: sleep deprivation, endless military tasks, drills, and training, along with incessant memorizations designed to test a candidate's ability to handle stress. But the payoff is sweet. Successful completion of PLC, coupled with graduation from college, means a commission in the United States Marine Corps—no small achievement for a twenty-two-year-old.

As Sullivan and McGyver described their summer and the challenge of PLC, their unbridled enthusiasm for their experiences sparked something in me that I recognized instantly—a newfound path for my life's direction. Their words were like a laser beam pointing the way. After hearing all they had to say, I thought to myself, *These two guys are building a future for themselves, and I have to know more about it.*

My motivation to serve was not inspired by any sense of family legacy, despite the fact that my dad and my older brother, Denis, had served in the Navy, and my uncle Jack and uncle Ralph had both been Marines. Quite honestly, I'd not given the armed forces much thought, much less serious consideration. The last time I had even thought about the military had been in 1983, after the terrorist bombing of the Marine barracks in Beirut. It was an incredibly sad day for America. I remember seeing the terrible images on TV, as young men pulled their fellow Marines from the rubble. It sickened me, and I would never forget it.

I wasted no time in contacting the Marine Corps, and on November 13, 1985, I boarded the train from New Rochelle to Manhattan to keep my appointment with the Marine Corps Selection Officer, Captain Stephen Cooperider. I had no idea what to expect. As I entered the building and walked past the Navy, Army, and Air Force recruiting offices, a chill of nervous excitement ran down my spine. Filled with anticipation, I quickly proceeded to the back of the building, where the sign on the door announced, *We make Marines here. If you think you have the mettle to be one of us, come in and learn more about the Few, the Proud, the Marine Corps.*

At 6'1", with an imposing physique and a commanding voice, Captain Cooperider was a larger-than-life poster Marine. He invited me into his office and put this college kid at ease as we talked at length about my decision to join and pursue a career in the Corps.

"Why are you here today?" he asked me point-blank. "Did you come here for yourself, or for someone else—your dad or brother, maybe?

Are either of them in the military? Why do you want to be a Marine? What do you know about the Marine Corps? What do you hope to accomplish?"

I sat up straight, cleared my throat, and as assertively and confidently as I could, said, "I want to be a part of the best military organization in the world, and I know the Marines are the best. I'm here because I want to be a Marine."

Cooperider wasn't impressed—or if he was, he certainly didn't show it. He quickly made it clear to me that the Marine Corps wasn't looking to hire just help; the Corps needed committed leaders. As Cooperider explained, the PLC program gives candidates the opportunity to see if they have what it takes to be leaders. "We'll be testing, challenging, and evaluating you to see if you have the leadership, integrity, intestinal fortitude, and character we want as a leader in our Corps." He made it perfectly clear about what would be expected of me and there was no doubt in my mind that he meant every word it.

He had my undivided attention and total interest as he went on to explain that if a candidate successfully completed the ten-week PLC program and four years of college, the Marine Corps would make him an offer to be a leader of Marines as a commissioned officer. "If you choose otherwise," said Cooperider, "we'll thank you for giving us your best effort and send you on your way."

As I walked back to Penn Station amid the jostling mid-day crowds, I could barely contain myself. There was no question; I wanted in. I wanted to take the challenge. I wanted to prove to myself, my family, and my friends that I had what it took to accomplish something so few people in our country could. For the first time in my adult life, I felt I had clarity of purpose. But more than that, I was energized and sure of one thing: I had to get back to Iona and get myself ready for what would clearly be the rigors—and, hopefully, the rewards—of PLC. I just had so much to do!

Not long after the interview, Captain Cooperider sent a letter to my parents recommending me for the following summer's Platoon Leader Class. "Robert impresses me with his high degree of self-confidence and strong sense of personal integrity," he wrote. "I am confident he would serve well in officer training." My parents were pleasantly shocked. Though they had always believed that I had it in me to "take the bull by the horns" and be successful at something, they never imagined I'd set my sights as high as attempting to become a Marine Corps officer. It was a tall order for sure, especially for someone once called the most unambitious kid in the world. And after answering all their questions about the program and assuring them that I knew what I was doing, I could see that they were very proud of me, especially my dad.

Later that night, my father pulled me aside to talk privately. "Your uncle Ralph was a Marine staff sergeant who served this country in Korea. I've always had great respect him. Everyone knows the Marines are the toughest of the military services. This isn't going to be easy, Bob, but I'm really proud of you for taking the initiative to attempt this path. Give it your best shot, son, and well done."

I was approved for the PLC program at Quantico's Officer Candidate School the following June. From that point on, a sense of immediacy overtook me and dominated all that I did. Unlike in years past, my focus was knife-sharp. I spared no effort in preparing myself physically, mentally, and academically. I studied intently for every exam, signed up for extra classes to take over the Christmas break, and made every attempt to run at least three miles a day. The intensity of my plans to join the Marine Corps, coupled with my newfound commitment to "get the job done" in one coordinated ten-week pass, marked the beginning of a leadership style that would prove invaluable, time after time, over the course of my career.

I said good-bye to my parents on June 9, 1986, before I boarded a plane for Washington DC and then a bus headed for Virginia and the Marine Corps base at Quantico.

For any PLC/OCS student, the routine is grinding and demanding. It's been known to take its toll on even the toughest candidates, and those who arrive at the school without any understanding of the military can find themselves behind the curve from the get-go. After the initial shock of realizing you're no longer home and you're certainly not in charge of anything going on around you for at least the next seven out of ten weeks (because the PLC program mandates that you must stay enrolled for at least that long before being allowed to drop or quit), you adjust rapidly to the intense, relentless routine. And though I had no idea how to press camouflage utilities, sing cadence, or spit-shine boots,

I was smart enough to either figure it out for myself or ask the prior enlisted candidates for help.

Make no mistake about it, though—I took my lumps. I would often joke in letters home to my parents that "I am one of the most popular officer candidates in my platoon. The platoon sergeant and sergeant instructors seem to be spending an inordinate amount of time with me." Translation: I was getting more than my fair share of "in your face" time from angry drill instructors trying to test my mettle. I don't know what it was, because I did my best to keep a low profile—to blend in—but somehow, my name would be the one shouted out, again and again, in the barracks, in the chow hall, and across the training fields. There seemed to be no respite; some mornings, I was in trouble within the first three minutes after getting out of the rack ... and most mornings started at 4:45 AM!

I hit a serious low point in July, about midway through my training. It was an incredibly hot, humid, typical Quantico summer day when I received a marginal grade on an important weapons exam. Immediately after, we were ordered to quickly pick up our gear and file out of the classroom for field training. My mind, still dwelling on my marginal academic performance, must have caused my body to hesitate at the drill instructor's last command. Suddenly, without warning, I found myself face-to-face with the ugliest, meanest, angriest Marine who ever walked the planet. He started waving his arms, pointing his hands, and spitting out incoherent words as he nearly pushed his own eyes from their sockets. I was frozen with fear. If I could have simply clicked my heels three times like Dorothy in *The Wizard of Oz* and awakened myself from that bad dream, I would have. But it wasn't a dream, and I definitely wasn't in Kansas.

I instinctively locked my body at attention, looked straight ahead, yelled "Yes, Sergeant Instructor!" and prayed this one-way exchange would end before any of the other drill sergeants from the other platoons started smelling the proverbial blood in the water and decided to rush over and join in on the kill. Fortunately, I survived—or at least I hoped I had. With my body still locked at attention and my eyes looking straight forward, he quietly moved behind me, disappearing from my view for what seemed like forever.

What is he doing back there? I thought silently. I remained frozen at the position of attention. I knew he was waiting for me to move or flinch without permission, so he could pounce once again. I wouldn't fall for it. Not this time. Slowly, he appeared in my peripheral vision on the right side of my body, as if examining every pore on my face.

He moved in close to my right ear and softly whispered, "You'd better fix yourself, Candidate, 'cause from here on out, I got both eyes on you." And he turned away and departed. It was over. I quickly gathered myself, shook off the looks from my fellow candidates, and returned to my usual place in formation, back in the third squad, third platoon. I took a deep breath and pressed on. *That was painful.*

Next stop, the infamous Leadership Reaction Course, or LRC—a maze of nearly unsolvable critical-thinking exercises designed to test one's ability to lead others, react under pressure, and to improvise with ingenuity … all in a race against time. There were approximately fifteen to twenty different stations, each with an equally challenging but different scenario for testing teamwork, intelligence, physical strength, and resourcefulness. Each team was made up of five or six officer candidates.

Our first exercise was in a mock prison yard surrounded by a minefield. We were given a steel six-foot ladder and a six-foot piece of rope. Our objective was to beat the clock and get our combat team across the minefield (the muddy pool of water about five feet long and three feet wide), and over the brightly painted red, five-foot wooden prison wall without touching any of the red areas with any part of our ladder, our equipment, or our bodies. If we so much as grazed the red areas in any way, we failed the challenge and were considered dead. The only portion of the wall that wasn't painted red was the very top and a three-foot-long two-by-four board nailed across the middle, about halfway up from the bottom.

Somehow, we needed to successfully lower the steel ladder down across the minefield and get it to land on the two-inch-wide edge of the two-by-four. If we overshot the landing, we would hit the red area on the wall and be considered dead. If we undershot the two-by-four and missed the board altogether, we obviously would fall into the minefield and fail as well. But if we could somehow figure out a way to do it, we could then use the ladder as a walking bridge to cross over the minefield

10

and jump over the prison wall. Marine instructors waited on platforms above us to ensure we followed the rules and to monitor our allotted time.

With the sound of a whistle, we went into action. One team member quickly assumed command and began issuing orders to the rest of us. When his strategy or plan failed due to someone inadvertently hitting the minefield, a second member of our group would assume command. This continued either until one of us led our team to a successful conclusion or until we all failed the challenge.

After the third member of our team failed, I took my turn at the helm. I ordered two team members to hold the steel ladder straight up, so I could climb to the top of it. I quickly tied our rope to the top rung and ordered the team to secure the bottom of the ladder with their feet and, with the rope in their hands, slowly lower me down, as on a drawbridge, toward the prison wall over the mock minefield. As the ladder got lower, I slowly moved myself down the rungs of the ladder toward the first rung to help lessen the strain of my weight on the others.

As the team continued to lower the ladder with me on it, my weight became heavier and harder to control, and soon it became too difficult to support. The ladder, with me still on it, began falling toward the "no touch" zones on the prison wall. It looked as if I, too, was headed for disaster. I was either going to hit the red areas on the wall or bounce off the two-by-four and fall into the minefield. Either way, I would fail.

The ladder slammed the two-by-four hard, but perfectly, and somehow it stayed in place. We all just froze. No one wanted to jeopardize our good fortune and cause the ladder to shift in any direction. Even the other Marine instructors, hearing the commotion, came running over to see what was happening and to double check that we had legitimately gotten that far into the challenge. We now had our bridge in place to get our team over the minefield, but time was rapidly running out.

Next we had to get our team over the prison wall. Under the careful eye of the Marine instructor above us, each team member quickly crossed over the bridge, and together, we threw the first member over the wall without touching the red zones. He was free! Within seconds, we had two out, and then three members were successfully out. With only two members now left inside, we thought that we were home free … until they blew the whistle.

Our time was up, and with two of us still inside the prison wall, it looked as if we had failed the exercise. *Oh, no,* I thought, *here comes another substandard grade.*

The Marine captain called our group together for our debriefing. To our amazement, we all received a 99 percent for the exercise—the highest grade given all day. According to the captain, no other group had been able to get anyone out of the prison, and we had freed three out of the five of us. The leadership and teamwork we displayed as a unit was the best he'd seen thus far. We had done it! It was amazing how quickly fortunes could change. I had gone from my lowest point to suddenly feeling as if I could do anything.

Many more challenges and even tougher days remained during my time at Quantico. But through it all, I never lost my sense of humor or my sense of purpose, and I remained friendly and popular with the other candidates, ultimately performing where it mattered most—leadership. Whether I was at the front of the pack sprinting over obstacles or through reaction courses and tactical field exercises, my leadership grades were some of the highest in the platoon. It was something I truly enjoyed … and actually seemed pretty good at!

At the completion of my training at OCS, the Marine Corps had transformed me both mentally and physically and enabled me to reach far beyond my personal comfort zones to succeed, not as an individual, but as an integral member of an elite team capable of accomplishing anything. They taught me that my attitude will always say more about me than my words; that quitting is never an option; and that there's no greater honor in life than to lead Marines in the defense of this great nation.

And so, on August 15, 1986, in front of family and friends, I proved I could hang with the best and graduated from Bravo Company, Third Platoon, on Quantico's sprawling parade ground on the Potomac. Generations of Marines, many of whom are buried at Quantico's nearby National Cemetery, had stood on the very ground where I was standing. From there, they had embarked on missions to the four corners of the world to defend our nation and, even more generously, to protect others from our enemies. I was proud to share that same soil with Marines who had taken Iwo Jima, who had persevered at Korea's Chosin Reservoir, and who had courageously fought at Ia Drang in Vietnam.

Twenty-four years later, I still insist that OCS was the single greatest accomplishment in my life. Not only did I emerge with a new and improved outlook, I arrived back home that August seventeen pounds lighter and feeling like a new man. Everyone, it seemed—from family, friends, and neighbors to my girlfriend and future wife, Angela—was impressed with the change in me and mentioned it again and again. And like my buddies Sullivan and McGyver the summer before, I found myself on the receiving end of questions from more than a few Iona classmates who came up to me. "Hey, what happened to you?" they would ask. And I was more than happy to tell them.

As I look back on the value of that experience, of bringing a bunch of guys together and exercising time-honored leadership principles, I conclude that serving in the military was a natural course for me. Thanks to the PLC program, for the first time in my young adult life, I felt grounded and sure about my future.

Back at Iona, the push was on for me to make up credits if I wanted to meet my goal of graduation and commissioning by the end of the school year. With the Quantico experience energizing and driving my every move, I put my face in my books, pressed hard, and earned my degree in economics in the spring of 1987.

ROBERT J. DARLING, UNITED STATES MARINE

I received my commission on June 6, 1987, aboard the mighty and historic USS *Intrepid* moored on the Hudson River in Manhattan, New York. It was an incredibly proud moment for me and my entire family. Over the next twenty-eight months, I went on to The Basic School (TBS) and flight school in Pensacola, Florida, and in the fall of 1989, I was promoted to first lieutenant, winged a naval aviator, and selected to fly the fearsome AH-1W Cobra Attack helicopter.

CHAPTER 3

My Road to the White House

MARINE CORPS LEADERSHIP EXPERIENCE

In the spring of 1993, I was deployed to the Horn of Africa with the Twenty-fourth Marine Expeditionary Unit (MEU), as part of the U.S. presence off the coast of Somalia. I had a chance to see, up close and personal, the disintegration of Somalia's society as Somali leadership, once friendly to the United States, turned dark and corrupt.

After six weeks of aerial escort and security missions for the United Nations forces, our MEU departed Somalia for the Persian Gulf to take part in Eager Mace—an annual joint exercise designed to strengthen the military coordination between the United States and our Persian Gulf allies. It was there, above the dark desert sands of Kuwait that my copilot and I would be credited with saving the lives of our two wingmen.

BUT FIRST: THE ORIGIN OF MY CALL SIGN

Trivia question: do you remember the name of Tom Cruise's character in the iconic movie *Top Gun*? It was Lt. Pete Mitchell. But you can be forgiven for not knowing that because of a long-standing tradition of assigning call signs to Navy and Marine pilots. You and millions of other filmgoers probably knew Cruise better by his call sign, Maverick—who flew with Goose, feuded with Iceman, and drove his instructor, Viper, crazy. Call signs evoke romantic images of cloud-splitting derring-do, hard loving, and even harder drinking among the fleet's elite birdmen. But, as many real-life pilots know, those celluloid jet jockeys and their widescreen exploits sometimes pale in the face of the real thing. There is nothing more real than war—service and sacrifice on battlefields that stand as precipitous bridges between life and death.

What you might not know is that call signs are not chosen; they're given by a pilot's peers—sometimes ceremoniously, sometimes ignominiously. However they come about, there's a story behind every one of them, and it has nothing to do with how good a pilot you think you are.

Mine was Shyster, a name bestowed on me in Saudi Arabia during the first Gulf War. In 1991, the Iraqi army was poised to push farther south from Kuwait into Saudi Arabia, and the world was on edge as the American-led Alliance and Saddam Hussein squared off for the fight. As my squadron sat at the Dhahran Airbase, preparing to go into battle, the word went out that the squadron commanding officer (CO) was in need of an adjutant, or aide, to help him manage his administrative responsibilities. Normally, this type of position was held by a junior officer because of the type of work it involved. For reasons unknown to me, out of the eligible twenty or so junior officers, I was chosen for the job. So, in addition to preparing myself to tactically fly and fight the Cobra helicopter, I was now responsible for keeping track of the CO's appointments, transportation needs, briefing materials, and on and on. I was counted on to be his "extra set of eyes and ears" in all matters regarding the health and morale of the squadron.

When the CO needed a sounding board to bounce an idea off, or someone to talk through a problem with, I was the one he confided in. This close and direct access to the CO, and the inside information I possessed, made me the junior officer every senior officer wanted to know better. And I knew it.

Unfortunately, the other junior officers in the squadron—my peers and my buddies—couldn't help but be resentful of my newly elevated status. And truth be told, maybe there was an occasion or two (okay, maybe three ... or possibly four at most) where I might have bragged a little too much that I had somewhere way cool to go, or that I had the inside track on information I wasn't at liberty to discuss, but which everyone wanted to know. Well, to my chagrin, I found out the hard way that what goes around comes around.

In the Cobra and Huey helicopter community, there's a traditional ceremony called the Cobra Court. It's a semiformal event—or more accurately, a beer fest—where junior officers stand and face other more senior officers in the squadron and officially receive their call signs. And unlike the always awesome names that come from the pens of Hollywood screenwriters, real-life call signs can be positive or negative, flattering or demeaning. They're usually tied to something you have, or lack, in physical nature. Sometimes they relate to a prominent character trait or perhaps something related to an incident that was an embarrassment in your professional or private life.

When it was my turn to face my fellow pilots, I made a fast and furious last-ditch sales pitch to convince them to call me Jedi, Maverick, Assassin, or Snake, but my lobbying only seemed to incite the crowd and make matters worse. The room erupted again and again with shouts of "Politician!" "Brown-noser!" "Teacher's Pet!" "Cabin Boy!" and still others not suitable for print. This loud, beer-fueled exchange went on for several minutes before the court was again called to order.

At these events, the court judge, normally the squadron executive officer, renders his "sentence," or call-sign decision, based on the preferences of the court's majority. This rendering is final, irrefutable, and irreversible for as long as you wear the wings of gold on your flight suit and remain a member of the attack-helicopter community. Although I hoped for the best, the raucous recommendations I heard coming from the drunk and angry crowd made me certain the decision wasn't going to be particularly flattering.

The judge then pronounced, "Of the many recommendations I've heard offered for First Lieutenant Darling, the word 'politician' seems to stand out most. His uncanny ability to work a crowd, to place himself in just the right place at the right time, and to always come out of downright dirty situations smelling like the proverbial rose leaves me to wholeheartedly agree with that characterization.

"But," he continued, "as members of the world's finest fighting force, we pride ourselves on being anti-political, meaning we're here to defend democracy, not to practice it. Therefore, I am left no choice but to render a suitable synonym for 'politician.'"

He then rendered his decision: "Let it be said that from here on out, Lt. Darling, you'll forever be known as Shyster." The crowd and my so-called friends went wild!

Lt. Scott Bailey was first to approach me to rub it in. "It couldn't have turned out any better than that," he said. "What is it they say about payback?" And with a big smile and a vindicated pat on my shoulder, he was gone.

Obviously, when you consider the definition of the word "shyster" (a lawyer who uses unprofessional or questionable methods), it does seems incredibly degrading and harsh, if not downright embarrassing, to have such a label attached to you, but the truth is that I never took it personally. I have always looked at it as more of a reflection of how we in the military viewed the behavior of many of our politicians back home at the time. I just so happened to be the one who bore that resentment.

Some of the other call signs awarded that night included van Gogh for the lieutenant who had his ear torn off while wrestling in the parking lot; Beetle for Lt. Bailey; and Irish, Screamer, Rabbi, Pisser, Roid, and so on, all for various and sundry reasons. I think you get the idea. Although my call sign wasn't even close to the cool name I was hoping for, I've always worn it with pride.

THE DARK SANDS OF KUWAIT

On June 9, 1993, as a newly promoted Marine captain, I led a division of Cobra Attack helicopters on a night training mission out to Kuwait's Udairi Range, located in the northwest corner of the country.

Flying in the desert in the daytime is challenging enough, but flying in the desert at night, even with the aid of night-vision goggles called NVGs, can be incredibly difficult and dangerous. One reason is the combination of the very fine sand and the often windy conditions that you find in the Persian Gulf region. This environment can often create sand dunes as high as one hundred feet or more. Add in the low altitudes and high rates of speed that attack helicopter pilots fly at, as well as having your wingman just fifty feet or so to the left or right of you, and you have one of the most dangerous environments a pilot can face. The only thing more challenging or dangerous would be to do it in actual combat.

On this particular moonless night, flying just above the pitch-black, featureless desert, our mission was to deliver 20-millimeter cannon rounds and high explosive rockets on a target the size of a family station wagon.

My copilot was First Lieutenant Ken Manny, call sign Kid. As his call sign suggests, Ken was a young, baby-faced Marine on his first deployment to the Persian Gulf. Lucky for me, though, he was an absolute professional—meticulous in his planning, with a stone-cold, inside-and-out understanding of the procedures.

In my wingman's aircraft were the pilot in command, Captain Tom Matkin, call sign Box, and his copilot, Captain Wally Adamcheck, call sign Irish. They were just as professional, and even more experienced at flying the Cobra helicopter than Kid. Once we got to the Weapons Delivery Range, I checked in with the Forward Air Controller (FAC), call sign Fish. The FAC is the marine on the ground manning the radio to ensure the training is executed safely and the weapons are always fired headed in the right direction. The FAC is the undisputed boss, and no one drops any bombs or shoots any ordnance without his approval. Fish briefed us on conditions at the range, including wind direction and speed, other air or ground traffic, and hazards such as wandering camels, as well as our target location.

It was dark—really dark. Even with the help of my NVGs, I could barely see my wingman. The radio crackled to life with the disembodied voice of Fish, giving us our run-in heading and ordering us to hold our fire until he cleared us "hot," a term used by aviators to mean that you are safely clear of friendly forces and are permitted to arm your weapons systems and fire your ordnance at the target once you have it in your sights.

I was at five hundred feet, beginning my descent to our minimum permitted altitude of two hundred feet. This altitude had been established to ensure we were always flying above known obstacles—things like telephone poles or communication towers—in the range complex. More importantly, it prevented us from driving our aircraft into the ground in an environment where there was very little contrast between the sky's horizon and the desert floor. Even with the aid of NVGs, it was difficult to see much detail and tell the depth of the objects I was looking at. Though the NVGs did enable me to see through the darkness, they only provided a very narrow, forty-degree field of view. It was the equivalent of looking through a toilet paper roll and seeing only a flat, glowing green picture of the desert floor—while traveling at over 110 miles per hour.

Kid was in the front seat searching for the target. I was in the back trying to maintain heading, altitude, and airspeed, when I finally had to call us "off cold," meaning our weapons system had been rendered safe, by moving our master arm switch from the Arm position to the Safe position, because we couldn't find our target. My wingman, Box, also reported "off cold" and followed behind us.

We regrouped at an aerial holding area away from the target and began commenting over the radio about how dark it was—a near pitch-black environment. As the section lead, I decided it would be safer for all of us if we put more distance between our aircraft to lessen the possibly of an in-flight collision with each other, given the extreme environmental conditions.

"Box, we need to put more separation between our aircraft."

"Roger," he acknowledged and slid his aircraft farther back off my right side, to the five o'clock position, maneuvering behind me.

I radioed Fish. "We're ready to push toward the target area again."

Fish immediately cleared us inbound. This time, Kid found the target in his gun sights, reported the aircraft wings level, and requested to be cleared hot.

"You are cleared hot," Fish replied.

Within seconds, the aircraft weapons systems screamed to life. The trace smoke from the rapid firing of our 2.75-inch folding-fin high-explosive rockets seeped into the cockpit air vents while white flashes from the powerful 20-millimeter cannon lit up the night sky. It was quite an impressive sound and light show.

We had unleashed a large salvo on that pass; as Fish reported "awesome hits," we called "off cold," with our weapons system safe.

As we again headed toward the holding area, we could hear Box report, "Target in sight, wings level," followed by Fish giving him the "cleared hot" and "good hits" call as they pulled off the target.

We were on a roll; the mission was going as planned.

I decided to move our aircraft into a racetrack attack pattern and give ourselves even more separation. The racetrack attack pattern was designed to put the maximum distance between aircraft in a training environment so pilots could focus solely on their weapons-delivery skills and not worry about having to maintain their position within a flight.

Box moved to a position that was 180 degrees apart from me—essentially on the opposite side of the aerial racetrack.

Fish radioed in, "Hey, Shyster, we've got an 81-millimeter mortar team that wants to provide overhead illumination of the target for your next pass." It was a stroke of luck. Having a million-candlepower flare floating down over the target area would enable us to see the target well enough to annihilate it. I immediately accepted the offer and almost immediately, Fish cleared us to proceed toward the target.

Kid and I were about thirty seconds from the target when the 81-millimeter flare fired and illuminated the entire target area. The white light was intense—far brighter than I had anticipated. The flare completely washed out my NVGs; the outside light was so bright that the goggles essentially ceased to function. For a brief moment, I was totally blinded. I tore the NVGs off my face and brought my scan inside the cockpit to see my flight instruments. I began monitoring my heading, altitude, and airspeed solely from inside the aircraft.

Over the intercom, Kid announced, "Hey, Shyster, I'm washed out—can't see a thing."

He had raised his goggles as well and was attempting to locate the target without his goggles when we heard the loud and urgent *whoop-whoop* of the low-altitude alarm! The low-altitude alarm is an onboard emergency system designed to alert the pilots when the aircraft descends below a preset altitude. That night, it had been set for two hundred feet above the ground. I instinctively leveled the aircraft and added maximum power to arrest my rate of descent, so we wouldn't bust the two hundred-foot minimum hard deck. We certainly didn't want to find ourselves flying nearly blind below the safe obstacle-avoidance altitude.

I turned away from the target area and reported us off cold, so Kid and I could regroup inside the cockpit. We were both taken aback by the blinding effects the powerful parachute flare had on our NVGs and how quickly we had become overwhelmed in the cockpit as we switched from "goggles on" to "goggles off" and tried to visually acquire the target.

We'd have to try again on our next pass. As we flew out of the flare's illumination field, Kid and I again lowered our goggles.

I heard Box's voice on the radio: "Target in sight." Fish cleared him hot. From our position, 180 degrees out from Box's, we could see his aircraft unleash its powerful payload. The exploding rockets and tracers from the Cobra's 20-millimeter cannon again made for an incredible sight.

And then came the scream!

Box and Irish were yelling into their microphones, "Holy shit! Holy shit! We hit something; oh, my God, we hit something!"

I quickly turned inbound to find out what had happened to my wingman. Clearly, from the transmission, they were still alive and airborne and not on the desert floor. I yelled to Kid to keep an eye out for them. When we got to the target area seconds later, we looked up and were stunned to see their Cobra rapidly climbing vertically at what seemed like full power, with no forward airspeed. Apparently, the sound of their rockets and guns blazing at the target had deafened them to the emergency tone of the low-altitude warning alarm, signaling that they had passed below the two hundred-foot hard deck.

According to Fish, it appeared that they'd flown their aircraft right through the top of a large sand dune and literally bounced off the desert floor. The impact of the collision apparently caused their attitude indicator to fail and their NVGs to snap off their helmet mounts. They were momentarily out of control and flying nearly blind.

Kid and I tried to catch up with them and join them in formation, but we couldn't because they weren't going forward, just straight up. To say this was not good would be an understatement. A pilot in a full-power, vertical-climb situation, at night, without the aid an outside reference or a working attitude indicator, could potentially lose all situational reference to the ground and, in turn, lose control of his aircraft.

At this juncture, I was sure of one thing: I had to get them to calm down, reduce power, level off, and put forward airspeed back on the aircraft. They were already passing two thousand feet and still climbing. They were obviously scared. I radioed Box and, as calmly as I could, told him I was with him, but that he had to reduce power, lower the nose of the aircraft, and *stop climbing!* As I pulled up underneath them, I could see that the damage to their aircraft was severe.

"Shyster," came his shaken voice over the radio, "I can't. I can't bring myself to do it. I can't."

At that point, Box was still too scared to do anything to help his cause. To make matters worse, Irish apparently was also flying the aircraft from the front seat. Both pilots were making inputs to the flight controls and flying at the same time, with neither one able to let go of the aircraft and allow the other to pilot the helicopter. Essentially, each had frozen at the controls, unable to disengage from the overpowering fear that had a bear-hold on the two of them.

I decided the best course of action at that moment was to keep talking to them and to let them know they'd be just fine; however, with each passing minute, I also knew that the possibility existed that the aircraft was so severely damaged from impacting the ground, it could fail at any moment and crash. I had to get them back to Kuwait International if they were going to survive.

Flying a helicopter is a full-body effort; you employ both hands and both feet in what is, essentially, a ballet of motion that is extremely unforgiving of errors. Doing that dance in a multi-million dollar attack helicopter, with its undercarriage stripped away, at night, without a clear field of vision and with rapidly diminishing fuel, involves high stress and even higher danger.

Slowly, with firm urging and as much patience as I could muster under the circumstances, I managed to relax Box enough for him to reacquire his composure and begin arresting his ascent, assessing his condition, and regaining some semblance of control over his damaged Cobra. Although it seemed as if it took forever, only a few minutes passed before Box had gotten himself, Irish, and their aircraft back in the game.

"Hey, Shyster, how does the aircraft look from your view?"

Box was coming to grips with what had happened and trying to get a handle on the extent of the damage to his aircraft.

I paused, wondering if he was mentally prepared for the news that the helicopter appeared to be heavily damaged. The landing skids were torn off, the rocket pods were missing, and the gun housing unit was broken and mangled. Additionally, a huge wire bundle swung wildly beneath the belly of the aircraft. I didn't want to rattle him any more than he already was, so I decided to turn his question around and ask about the one all-important gauge of survivability at the moment. "Box, how's it handling? Is it responding to your control inputs?"

"The instrument console lights are out, and the front seat attitude gyro is broken, but both engines and the flight controls seem to be functioning okay."

"Good," I said, trying to insert something—anything—positive into the mix. "You guys are going to be all right, but we'll have some serious work to do when we get on the ground."

"So, Shyster, how bad is it?" Box asked again, his voice tentative and apprehensive.

"Considerable damage, Box." A heavy silence followed as Box took in the bad news. I could only imagine what he was thinking. There's nothing worse for a pilot than to lose or damage his aircraft. The responsibility for the life of your crew and the multi-million dollar equipment under your charge is enormous.

"Seriously, Shyster, are my skids still there?"

"I'm sorry, Box … totally gone. The bottom of your aircraft is as smooth as a baby's ass. We need to get back to Kuwait International ASAP. They'll have all the emergency equipment we need to get the aircraft on the ground safely."

Box agreed. Like all of us that night, he was committed to making the best of a bad situation.

Kid, as usual, was one step ahead of me and had already mapped out the proper heading, distance, and radio frequencies for both Kuwait approach control and tower.

Box and Irish seemed more self-possessed with each passing minute, and so we were on our way. Now, I just hoped their badly damaged Cobra would stay together and keep flying long enough for me to figure out a plan to get them on the ground. Fifty-six miles was a long way to go in an aircraft that could lose total electrical power or suffer a major system shutdown at any moment. As we progressed toward the airport, I was relieved to hear that Box and Irish had started talking to each other. It was another good sign.

I overheard Irish bulleting a series of questions. "How much fuel do we have right now? Do you think we can land using just the wing stubs? Do you think they'll support the weight of the aircraft?"

This went on for a few more seconds until I heard Box finally say in a very slow, calm, and measured voice, "Wally, give me the controls. It'll be all right."

There was a brief silence before Wally released the controls and quietly acknowledged, "You have the controls, Box."

Finally, I thought. *Now we're making real progress!* But we certainly weren't out of the desert yet.

With both Cobras getting low on fuel, I told Kid to get on the radio to let the Kuwait tower know that we were coming toward them and that we needed some serious help.

The trip seemed endless. As we got closer to the airport, I felt the pressure of time bearing down on me. One question rolled over and over in my mind: How was I going to get this heavily damaged Cobra helicopter on the ground and shut down safely without its landing gear or skids? There was no way to simply land the helicopter on just its belly without the rotor forces causing it to tip over during shutdown. The impact of the main rotor on the ground would be catastrophic. That crash scenario replayed in my head as we silently made our way through the night sky toward the airport. I knew if that tragic scenario played out, there wouldn't be much hope for either Box or Irish to walk away uninjured, if even alive.

Kid and I contacted the Kuwait International Approach Control and told them we were a flight of two American helicopters, twenty miles out, and needed Crash, Fire, and Rescue to stand by. The approach controller spoke excellent English and understood our situation. At five miles out, he told us to contact the Kuwait tower. I did, and my stomach tightened when I realized the controller in the tower was clueless and could barely speak English.

"Kuwait Tower, this is Helicopter Flight XX approaching Kuwait International from the north, five miles out. We are a section of two

U.S. helicopters. My dash-two aircraft is badly damaged and needs immediate assistance from Crash, Fire, and Rescue; please advise."

I must have repeated that request a half dozen times, in as many different ways, to no understandable response that I could make out. He spoke only broken English and seemed to have no idea who we were or where we were. I wasn't all that sure he even had a grasp of the severity of our problem.

I was frustrated and angry, but above all, I was concerned that we wouldn't get the ground support we desperately needed to safely land Box's skid-less helicopter.

To my great relief, someone inside the Kuwait tower must have at least understood that there was one, maybe two badly damaged helicopters inbound somewhere from the north, because we could see the Crash, Fire, and Rescue trucks pull out of their garage with their emergency lights on and stop, as if they were awaiting further instructions. Well, that was all I needed to see. They didn't have to worry about finding me, because I flew right to them, while dangerously crossing over all the operating runways in the process.

While Box's aircraft hovered over the landing area, I put my Cobra down, jumped out, and told Kid to get out and find me the guy in charge.

"We need to find something for Box and Irish to land on!" I shouted as Kid ran off. The plan was to get some steel pallets, stack them four feet high, and set them just wide enough apart for Box to hover his aircraft over them and gently lower himself down until the entire weight of the aircraft was resting on the Cobra's wing stubs, keeping the belly of the aircraft off the ground

Our time to find these pallets was growing very short as Box radioed, "Shyster, I have less than fifteen minutes of fuel left."

The Kuwaiti fire chief approached, and we briefly discussed the situation.

I was shocked when he asked me if it was okay to use foam on the aircraft when it crashed and rolled over. Like me, he was tense and uptight, pressured by the grim immediacy of the situation; but unlike him, I wasn't about to write off Box and Irish with talk of a crash and rollover as the default answer to the fix we were in. There had to be another way.

"Yeah, if we have to," I quickly answered, "but we still have ten minutes to prevent that. Here's the drill." I explained the plan, but the chief said he had no idea where to find such pallets and proceeded to order his crew to back up and stand by.

I looked up and, amid the lights shining on Box's hovering helicopter, motioned to him that we were still looking for something for him to land on.

He held up his hand in response, indicating that he had only five minutes of gas left.

I was getting desperate. "Chief," I said, "can you let me have some equipment from the garage that could be set up to support the weight of the aircraft?"

"No, no, I'm sorry. We have nothing like that. We're not authorized to do that. We can't help you, Captain."

I was running out of patience with this guy, but I didn't have any more time to waste arguing with him. It was time to tell Box that we'd have to go to Plan B. He'd have to land the helicopter on its three and half foot wide belly and miraculously keep it upright as he shut down the engines and the enormous two thousand-pound main rotor began to slow and become unstable. Even the slightest wind gust could cause the main rotor to teeter and flip the helicopter onto its side, striking the ground. The impact with the tarmac would cause the helicopter to tumble and the main rotor to splinter into hundreds of pieces of flying shrapnel, potentially wounding or killing Box and Irish and others nearby as well.

I wished I could have traded places with them at that moment, but the truth is that Box was one of the very best pilots in the squadron. If anyone was capable of scoring a win out of this situation, it was him.

The Kuwaiti fire chief saw we were out of time and ideas and ordered all of his men to pull back. They would take up positions outside the crash zone and rush in to fight the fire and perform the rescue after all violent aircraft motion had come to a stop.

Just then, out of nowhere, came Kid driving a tow tractor across the tarmac at max speed, with two four-foot-high stacks of steel air force pallets trailing behind him. I couldn't believe it. I'd been hoping against hope, and here he'd actually done it! I wanted to start jumping up and down, hollering, but there wasn't time for that.

With literally seconds to spare, we moved the pallets into position, four feet apart, on either side of the hovering helicopter, and secured them with tie-down straps. I again turned to the Kuwaiti fire chief. "Chief, can you get one of your men to guide the copter in between the pal—"

He wouldn't let me finish, waving his hands as if it was too late for that and ordering his men to stay back away from the soon-to-land helicopter—as if it was an explosive ready to blow. *Thanks for nothing, Chief,* I thought to myself.

As the firemen departed, I grabbed the taxi wands from one of the firefighters and took up a position in front of the helicopter, where Box could clearly see me waving him forward between the pallets. As he centered the helicopter over the pallets, I gave the signal with my arms to lower the aircraft down.

With almost no time to spare, Box expertly maneuvered the Cobra ever-so-gently between the pallets and set his crippled helicopter's wing stubs down, directly on the pallets. They took the full weight of the Cobra without the slightest shift. The balance was perfect, and Box safely shut down the helicopter. The main rotor slowed and then stopped. Silence. It was the end of a long and harrowing night.

Box and Irish scrambled out of the helicopter and immediately hugged each other. It was an intense moment. As they turned toward Kid and me, we all practically tackled each other with overwhelming joy and relief. We knew what we'd just done. We knew how close we had come to disaster. We were all just so relieved that we were all alive and that it was over!

Later that night, Kid told me that he had run down to the main air terminal looking for the sturdy gear or pallets and, oddly enough, had come across a Marine Corps corporal on his way back to the States. Kid stopped him and quickly explained the situation and what he needed. Without a second's hesitation, the corporal jumped into action, knowing exactly which one of the airport's many hangars held the kind of pallets Kid described. Several American and Kuwaiti military personnel on duty pitched in to help the corporal and Kid load the pallets onto the tow in two four-foot high stacks. In short order, Kid was on his way back to the landing pad.

Kid never saw the corporal again and, unfortunately, as is often the case in fast-moving events, he never got his name. But had it not been for that U.S. Marine in a faraway country, on a foreign tarmac, with knowledge of where we could find just the type of pallets we needed, we wouldn't have been able to save Box and Irish.

Was it divine intervention, or were we just lucky? No one will ever know for sure. But one thing was clear: the crisis-leadership skills I learned at every level of my Marine training—from basic training at Quantico to flight training at Pensacola, to flying in one of the world's most fearsome helicopters in a Middle East combat zone during Desert Shield, Desert Storm, and in Somalia—all put me in good stead to meet the challenges that would lie ahead. I could have never guessed just how difficult, if not life-altering, some of those experiences would actually be.

I, obviously, also never imagined that my crisis-leadership ability would once again be put into action eight years later, in the basement of the White House, supporting our nation's highest leaders during a terrorist attack on our country.

After a few more very successful tours as an instructor pilot and officer recruiter, I received word that I had been selected to fly with the Nighthawks, Marine Helicopter Squadron One (HMX-1), the Marine Corps squadron that transports the President and Vice President of the United States. It was a plum assignment by any measure and a heady job for a newly promoted Marine major.

CHAPTER 4

WHITE HOUSE DUTY

The military's presence within the Executive Mansion boasts a long and distinguished history. It originated with General Washington's aide-de-camp, whose role as personal aide to the President has continued unbroken since Washington took office in 1789.

Today, the military performs a wide variety of functions at presidential events, from critical military command and control missions to ceremonial duties. Among the most mission-critical operations assigned to the military is the around-the-clock ability to transport the President and the Vice President wherever and whenever they need to go.

The helicopter crews of Marine Helicopter Squadron One (HMX-1), flying Sikorsky VH-3Ds or the newer VH-60Ns, are made up of the "best of the best" Marine pilots, chosen for their skill in meeting some of the most demanding transportation conditions in or out of the military. The precision with which these pilots maneuver their helicopters is tested in front of national and international audiences whenever the President arrives or departs from the White House and when he makes appearances around the country or around the world. Who hasn't seen the iconic images of America's leaders standing in the doorway of Marine One on the South Lawn?

I can say without hesitation that my experience with HMX-1 was incredible. Sure, I traveled all over the world, but better than that, I learned to fly the CH-53E Sea Stallion, along with the VH-60N and VH-3D Presidential aircraft, eventually working my way through the White House pilot syllabus and earning the designation of aircraft commander in all three aircraft.

One of my favorite memories of flying as the Marine One copilot for President Clinton was when we lifted off from a landing zone in Memphis, Tennessee. President Clinton personally came up on the intercom system to speak to us in the cockpit. *This is a bit unusual,* I thought. *He normally passes comments through his military aide.*

He said, "Hey, thanks for flying over Elvis's house—I had never seen it from this angle before!"

The pilot in command and I stared blankly at each other for a brief second. Then I jumped on the intercom and said, "Ah, yes, sir, Mr. President, I thought you might like that." And then the pilot and I both pressed our faces as hard as we could against the wind screen in an attempt to see Graceland for ourselves before it disappeared from view.

Another time, I picked up Vice President Gore at Andrews Air Force Base to bring him back to his residence at the Naval Observatory in Washington. The Vice President had been in New York the night before as a guest on *The Late Show with David Letterman.* Usually very quiet and reserved, he had been very funny on the show.

Though we, as pilots, are not supposed to engage our VIPs in any manner other than the customary, "Hello, Mr. Vice President," I decided to take a bit of a risk this particular time. As the VP came up the stairs of Marine Two and reached into the cockpit for the customary handshake, I said, "Hello, Mr. Vice President."

"Hi, how are you, Major?" was the quick reply.

But as he turned to find his chair, I held his handshake just a second longer and said, "Mr. Vice President, I thought you did a great job on *Letterman* last night."

At first he seemed somewhat startled, and as he turned and stared back at me, I thought, *Uh-oh, maybe I overstepped my bounds and shouldn't have done that.*

But then his face lit up with a huge smile and he looked me in the eye and said, "Hey, thanks, man—I really appreciate that!" When he saw that my copilot, Major Chip Rumsey, had a digital camera in his hand, he asked him if he'd like to take a picture of us right there in the cockpit. Vice President Gore then knelt down, put his arm around me, and posed for a picture.

The press corps outside the aircraft was frantically trying to switch to the zoom lenses on their cameras in an attempt to figure out what the heck was going on in the helicopter cockpit. It was a great moment.

But unfortunately, as with all things in life, things can change. One day in October of 2000, I was ordered to report to the squadron commanding officer. I had no idea why he wanted to see me. After I positioned myself at attention in front of his desk with the customary, "Reporting as ordered, sir," he quickly put me at ease and told me to take a seat.

"Major Darling, here's the situation. I need to assign a senior aviator to the White House Airlift Operations office to replace the outgoing HMX-1 helicopter pilot who just received orders to report to a new assignment in Monterey, California."

I could tell from his matter-of-fact delivery that he wasn't asking me to consider the assignment; he was simply informing me that I'd been picked for it, and that it was a done deal.

After the "Yes-sir-thank-you-sir" routine, I left the squadron commander's office feeling more than a little disappointed. I had truly been enjoying my time flying the presidential fleet helicopters so easily recognized by their distinctive white tops, and I especially enjoyed all the overseas travel. This new assignment meant a suit and tie—and, worse yet, no flying. What's more, I had no idea what an Airlift Operations liaison officer to the president's staff even did. *Damn!*

Within a week, I was in my new job in the White House Airlift Operations office—a high-profile, high-energy facility manned by representatives from each branch of the military and from every unit supporting the President. I was now the Marine Corps' representative from HMX-1. In other words, I was the new resident expert on presidential helicopter operations.

Airlift Operations is the logistics arm of the White House Military Office (WHMO). Its mission is to coordinate with the Department of

Defense for the safe and timely travel of the President, Vice President, first family, and other designated VIPs who work in direct support of the White House.

Part of the job included notifying the crews of Air Force One, Marine One, the White House Communications Agency (WHCA), and the Secret Service of the upcoming scheduled presidential events and to ensure that the Air Mobility Command (AMC) was prepared to transport them to their specific worldwide locations in time to fully advance and support the President's visit.

The office is headed by a full colonel or Navy captain who answers to the director of WHMO. On a weekly basis, each officer is assigned a specific VIP and takes responsibility for ensuring that individual's travel, whether local, national, or international. At the end of each week, the assignments rotate. This procedure prevents workload burnout and ensures that everyone is familiar with the specific logistical requirements and preferences of all VIPs in the rotation. This job had turned out to be seriously important work.

For the presidential trips, it was the preplanning that required a lot of work. Two to four weeks prior to a presidential trip taking place, the planning commenced. It involved meeting regularly with the White House travel staff to map out the logistical requirements for the presidential trip to include the number of events the President would be attending, the locations, the number of people traveling with him, whether he could be airlifted by helicopter or needed to travel by motorcade, and whether there was a suitable medical facility with Trauma One medical capability located nearby. For a hospital to be considered suitable, the medical center had to have trauma surgeons with specialties in both neurosurgery and orthopedic surgery. If there was no such facility available, I would have to add a White House medical team and their associated equipment to our logistics package.

Once the details were established, I put in an airlift request through the Department of Defense, Office of the Assistant Vice Chief of the Air Force, Special Assignment Air Mission Division, also known as CVAM. CVAM is the primary DoD unit manned to support the U.S. government airlift-mission needs for senior government officials. CVAM would then pass the information on to the Air Mobility Command at Scott Air Force Base, Illinois, with the date, type, location, and number of assets the White House needed to have airlifted to a particular site or location. For the Air Mobility Command, an airlift mission that supports the president is called a Phoenix Banner mission; the vice president, a Phoenix Silver mission; and if it's in support of the first lady, a Phoenix Copper mission.

SEPTEMBER 10, 2001

As the Airlift Operations officer responsible for the presidential missions that week, I organized and supported President Bush's trip to Florida on September 10, 2001, by arranging to have the Air Mobility Command airlift five hardened Secret Service cars, numerous pallets of communication gear, and more than two hundred support personnel from Andrews Air Force Base to Sarasota, Florida, a full four days prior to the President's scheduled arrival. This gave the members of the White House Military Office and the Secret Service plenty of time to rehearse every aspect of the event, to include traveling the primary and alternate motorcade routes, practice landing in and taking off from the predetermined helicopter landing zones, as well as knowing the locations of all the local hospitals and their level of trauma capability so that when the President arrived on Air Force One, everyone was fully trained and prepared to safely transport and protect him as he executed his political agenda.

As I watched Marine One lift the President from the South Lawn of the White House, I crossed my fingers and prayed that all went according to plan.

And it did, at least at first. The President was scheduled to come back to the capital the next day immediately following his visit to the Emma E. Booker Elementary School in Sarasota. It would be a quiet couple of days for me ... or so it seemed.

CHAPTER 5

A Morning Unlike Any Other

On the morning of September 11, 2001, I woke up in the home I shared with my wife, Angela, and our two young sons, Michael and Matthew, in Stafford, Virginia, a suburb about thirty miles south of Washington DC.

My alarm went off at 5:20 AM and then again at 5:30 AM. After forcing myself out of bed, I picked out a clean suit and got dressed. It was customary that military personnel who worked at the White House wore business attire to work rather than their military uniform, so the place would look less like a military base and more like the home of the first family. It was only on Wednesdays that we were permitted to show up wearing our specific military service uniform. For Marines, that usually meant wearing the Charlie uniform—the green trousers and tan short-sleeved shirt. In the winter months, we switched to a long-sleeved tan shirt with a tie, called the Bravo uniform. The exact reason why we permitted to wear our uniforms on Wednesday was a bit of a mystery, but it was also a welcome opportunity to display ourselves as the fighting men and women of America's armed forces, proud to serve both our country and our President.

By 6:00 AM, I was dressed and had slipped quietly out of the house and into my car, heading to Washington and the White House.

My first stop was the slug line. What other cities call "ride sharing" and "carpooling" is known in Washington's Virginia suburbs as "slugging," an informal, self-monitoring system that costs nothing and not only moves thousands of commuters to work every day, but does so faster than the bus, Metro, or train systems.

Slugging's randomly marked pickup/drop-off points are not announced or printed anywhere; they come under the heading of common knowledge in neighborhoods and central points around town. All in all, it's an efficient, functional, unconventional transportation system for commuters who otherwise would be forced to fend for themselves on some of the most congested commuter highways in the country. It's a mutually beneficial system, too. Riders get free transportation to work, and drivers get to transform their empty cars into high-occupancy vehicles (HOVs) and therefore earn the right to drive in Interstate 95's fast HOV lane.

At the commuter lot located just behind McDonald's on Route 610 in Stafford, Virginia, those looking for a ride formed two lines—one for the Pentagon and nearby locations and one for downtown DC. The Pentagon was on my way to work, and with so many people working on any given day, there was always a surplus of sluggers looking for rides. I drove slowly along the Pentagon slug line, and with my window rolled down, yelled out, "Two for the Pentagon … I'll take two for the Pentagon!"

In no time at all, I had the two passengers I needed. They were both female civilian employees at the Pentagon. They hopped into my car, greeted me with a grateful "hello," and we were off.

We sluggers had things down to a science. The passengers usually followed the lead of the driver. If he wanted to chat, they chatted. If not, no one would usually forced the issue. This was a useful accommodation, after all, not a social occasion. We were still three strangers, and it was only a little after seven in the morning. Unless something incredibly newsworthy had just happened the night before that overwhelmed my ability to keep my mouth shut—something like the Washington Redskins winning—I rarely engaged in lengthy conversation with my passengers.

That day was no different. As soon as I heard the click of their seat belts, I turned up the volume on my radio, pulled out of the commuter lot, and joined the madness on Interstate 95 North. One of my passengers read her newspaper; the other stared out the window, probably pondering the day ahead.

My day, I thought, was to be fairly straightforward and ordinary. President Bush was in Sarasota, Florida, on a trip designed to spotlight education and reading, and all I had left to do was make sure the Air Mobility Command had everything in place to bring the presidential gear home the moment the President was safely on his way home aboard Air Force One.

As I came up the Interstate 395 hill toward Washington that morning, right by the Army Navy Country Club, I was shocked at how bright the sun was and how unusually clear the nation's capital looked across the Potomac River. This was the view that gave me pause every morning, but that day, it was truly spectacular. The Pentagon was directly in front of me, and the dome of the Capitol was clearly visible in the distance to the right, as were all the monuments in between. Washington looked amazing.

This had to be the early fall weather reward the locals had earned by putting up with the heat and humidity in the summer. The skies were clear, the air was fresh, and the District of Columbia, glimmering in the sun's spotlight, looked so beautiful that I couldn't help but feel great. I smiled as I reminded myself that I worked at the White House, at the nerve center of America and in support of the most powerful man in the world, as a member of the most powerful military force in the world.

I exited the HOV lane at the Pentagon and entered the enormous Pentagon complex, following the signs for the passenger discharge area. The Pentagon was a city unto itself. On any given morning, literally thousands of people in uniform and in civilian clothes headed toward the building on foot from the enormous parking lots that surrounded it. They had come by car, by subway, or by public transportation, and they represented all walks of life and many different levels of responsibility— but, as a member of the military family, I always thought of them as unified by their mission: to defend America.

7:20 AM

I pulled over to let my passengers out, urged them both to have a nice day, and carefully began following the exit signs in hopes of making it out of there without accidentally running over one of the nearly twenty-seven thousand others heading for their cubicles in the building

I crossed over the Memorial Bridge and then, a few blocks later, pulled into one of the spots reserved for White House personnel along the Ellipse, the much-photographed park between the Washington Monument and the White House. I walked from there up to the 17th Street entrance of the Eisenhower Executive Office Building, otherwise known around town as the EEOB. It is the only building on the west side of the White House campus.

I scanned my badge, typed in my security code, and entered through the metal detectors, making my way to the Airlift Operations office on the fourth floor.

7:50 AM

The first one through the door each morning usually picked up the *Washington Post*, which got delivered to the door outside the office, and I guessed Air Force Major Andrew Cox had been first, since he was sitting at his desk, reading the paper, and eating the fruit and whole-wheat muffin he always brought in from home for breakfast.

With a quick, "Good morning, Drew," I dropped my briefcase, logged onto my computer, opened Internet Explorer, and began skimming some of my favorite news, finance, and sports Web sites.

"How about that Barry Bonds?" I asked Technical Sergeant Mike McMahon, the office sports enthusiast, as he walked in behind me. Bonds had hit three home runs in one game against Colorado two nights before, a feat that had lifted him over the magical record of sixty home runs in a season that Babe Ruth had set in 1927 and the sixty-one-home-run record Roger Maris had set in 1961.

"What a night for baseball that was," McMahon sighed, shaking his head. "I couldn't believe it. Three in one game."

"Just seven more home runs, and he'll beat Mark McGwire's record," I said.

"I wouldn't hold my breath on that one." Mike had an opinion on everything sports-related, and it didn't take him long to get on his soap box that morning. "Nah," he said, shaking his head, "He'll never beat McGwire's record."

"He's got plenty of time left in the season to do it," I continued.

"You wait—they'll walk him every time he gets up to bat," he said. "Seven home runs is a lot to hit when no one's willing to pitch to you. Besides, he can't handle a real pitcher. He can't hit Roger Clemens or Mariano Rivera." The six-time Cy Young Award winner Roger Clemens had just been featured on the cover of *Sports Illustrated* the day before and was on track to have one of his best seasons ever as a New York Yankee.

I grinned. "With more than twenty games left in the regular season, not to mention the playoffs," I said over my shoulder as I headed out to the first-floor cafeteria to get my much needed cup of coffee, "I'd say there's a real chance he'll do it."

When I returned, Dennis Stump, the Airlift Operations civilian deputy, a man of medium build with a full head of white hair and enormous experience when it came to Air Force operations, was at his desk, getting ready to review the day's events and discuss the upcoming airlift requirements.

8:10 AM

We all gathered around and looked up at the large, white magnetic board on the back wall that displayed all the Special-Assignment Air Missions, or SAAMs, that were either being executed or planned. Each VIP was represented by a different-colored magnet. Air Force One travel plans were depicted in blue, the president's helicopter missions in green, the vice president's in yellow, and the first lady's in pink. White House delegation trips were depicted on the board with a white magnet, and lastly, the Air Mobility Command logistic support missions appeared in grey. Each magnet had a number and a destination. Since nothing major was happening that day other than bringing the President back to DC, Dennis focused on the upcoming trips.

"Have we scheduled a pickup for Secret Service for next Wednesday's departure to New York?" Dennis asked.

"Yes, sir, that's taken care of," I replied.

"Which type of aircraft has been assigned?

"Two C-130s."

"Good."

"Do we know if a White House medical team is required for the President's upcoming trip to Guam?"

"Not sure yet," I told him. I'm going to look into that today." It was the second day of my weeklong duty supporting the President of the United States (or POTUS, as we referred to him), and I was looking forward to getting several things tied down.

The give-and-take was always amicable, but sober. We all paid close attention. Dennis Stump was no joke teller, but you could count on him to laugh at yours if it was worthy of a response. He seemed to appreciate a funny story or one-liner, but he was dead serious when it came to airlift operations for the President. If we missed the details of an upcoming event or were late with the scheduling or screwed up a manifest for Air Force One or Marine One, we knew we could count on Dennis getting "game day" serious with all of us.

Today, however, looked like the kind of uneventful day where we would all be able to get ahead of the game, calling our counterparts in the Secret Service Office and beginning the planning process for future events. The President was due to return from Florida, the Vice President was in the White House, the First Lady had commitments in and around DC, and there were no congressional delegation missions in the offing.

In addition, across much of the Eastern Seaboard, the weather was beautiful: sunny with ten miles of visibility; the outside temperature at any given location between seventy and eighty-two degrees; and winds at six to eight knots out of the northwest.

No one could know that at that very moment, four teams of terrorists were bearing down the East Coast from our New England capital … to our financial capital … to our political capital.

CHAPTER 6

THE ATTACK

And so it began.

At approximately 8:46 AM, American Airlines Flight 11 tore into the ninety-sixth floor of the North Tower of the World Trade Center.

Like most Americans who are old enough to remember that day, I will carry the events that followed for the rest of my life, seared into my memory. The difference was that I was about to watch them unfold deep within our government's nerve center—inside the White House bunker. I saw and heard firsthand the reactions and responses of our nation's leaders as the day passed in all of its minute-by-minute terror, with each event raw, unvarnished, and unfiltered by the speculations of glib news anchors.

The news of the first airplane hit on the World Trade Center reached the Airlift Operations office at about 8:50 AM and, like much of the country, we turned on CNN to get the details. Almost simultaneously, my wife, Angela, called to see if I heard the news about the plane crash in New York. "I just did," I told her, and thanked her for the "heads-up" call before hanging up. We all then stood in front of the television, speculating as to how and why an aircraft would have hit such a huge and prominent landmark on a crystal-clear morning. Had the pilot had a heart attack? Had some sort of massive aircraft technical failure occurred?

Technical Sergeant Michael McMahon was the first to speak up. "Guys, that was no small plane that made that huge gash," he said, almost as if talking to himself. "Maybe it was no accident."

"Oh, come on, Mike," one of us replied. "You've seen one too many disaster movies."

"No way, Mike," another agreed. "It's got to be an accident—a tragic accident."

As each of us took in the stunning image on the screen, I think we collectively discounted his thinking as just too unbelievable. Though no one was ready to make that leap then, it didn't take the rest of us long to agree with him.

At approximately 9:03 AM, staring at the TV, I commented to the others in the room as another airliner came into view. "Okay, so what's this moron doing?" *No doubt trying to get a close-up view of the hole in the building*, I thought to myself.

All of a sudden, to my horror and total disbelief, the airliner careened into the South Tower at what looked like full power, smashing with such fury that it looked as if the building wanted to fall over right then and there.

A chorus of shouts and yells filled the room.

"Holy shit, did you see that?"

"Oh, my God."

"No, I can't believe it!"

Then, dead silence.

Everyone watched in shock, absolutely stunned, as the inferno and billowing smoke poured from New York's signature monuments to its financial supremacy. We were only wrenched from our private thoughts when someone shouted, "There's a full-blown terrorist attack happening right before our eyes in New York City!"

Like so many others across the country who phoned family members, I quickly called my oldest brother, Sean, a bank manager at the First National Bank of Highland in Newburgh, New York, and told him to turn on the TV, because there was some kind of terrorist attack happening in New York City.

Just about then, Dennis Stump, our deputy director, called out, "Attention, everyone! Heads up. I want each of you to stand by for the probability of a lot of high-level, White House-directed airlift requests

44

that might start coming in support of the first responders in New York."

When tragedy strikes on a national level and emergency supplies have to get to a disaster site immediately to save lives, the White House usually steps in on behalf of another government agency, such as FEMA, and orders the DoD to take action and coordinate the Special-Assignment Air Missions necessary to support them. That's because when the White House orders it, it gets assigned as the highest priority mission code or designator, and it gets done ASAP. That's not always the case when another government agency contacts the DoD directly and requests airlift support; their priorities don't always trump a DoD priority, and days may pass before their mission takes place. All the Cabinet directors know that the "White House-directed" designation is a much more powerful force in getting things done than simply "agency-requested" label.

"I imagine calls will probably start coming in soon for military airlift support for New York. We need to—"

As Dennis was talking, the deafening noise of a low-flying, approaching airliner drowned out his voice as it overflew the EEOB and White House. We paused for a moment, staring at each other before running for the window. After having just watched the destruction in New York in real time, to say we were unnerved would be an understatement. A flyover like this was extremely unusual, because the airspace over the White House is classified as prohibited airspace, meaning no one is allowed to fly over it—ever.

Technical Sergeant Mike McMahon, who sat closest to the window, called out, "I just caught a glimpse of what looked like the tail of an airliner.... Look! Over there! It's in a hard left hand turn.... It's heading away from the White House." We now had the first inkling that this attack may not just be on New York, but on our nation's capital as well.

Within minutes, CNN announced more breaking news and switched its attention from the World Trade Towers in New York City to inform us that they were now receiving reports of a large explosion and significant fire at the Pentagon. As I struggled to process what I had just heard and what I was now seeing on the news, my phone rang. It was Angela, again.

"What's going on, Bob?" This time her usually low, calm voice was direct and tense. "Is it true the Pentagon was just hit? The news reports say a plane slammed into it, just like in New York. Bob, I'm with Christine, and she's very upset. She can't reach Tom."

Tom was an Air Force lieutenant colonel who worked in the Pentagon. Christine was unable to reach him, because all of the cellphone airwaves were jammed. Of course, I had no idea if Tom was okay or not; I wasn't even sure if I was all right at the moment. I told Angela I didn't have any details on what the situation was at the Pentagon, but that I'd call her back as soon as I knew something definitive. As I hung up, I couldn't help but wonder whether the plane that had just flown over the White House was the one that just crashed into the Pentagon. If so, had the White House been the intended target? Were more attacks coming? Just what the hell was going on?

9:45 AM

What happened next was even more unbelievable. The building's intercom suddenly came to life and ordered all personnel to evacuate the White House and the adjoining Eisenhower Executive Office Building.

"Evacuate the White House complex! All personnel are to evacuate the White House complex immediately ... Evacuate the White House complex! All personnel are to evacuate the White House complex immediately!"

When in our history was the last time something like that ever happened? Dolly Madison, maybe, rushing from the White House carrying out what she could as the British closed in on the city? Things were happening so fast that my mind raced to catch up and process this series of incredible events.

As we secured our work spaces and prepared to leave the building, I grabbed Colonel Mike Irwin, our Director of Airlift Operations. I discussed with him the possibility that the President wouldn't be coming back to Washington that day, and as the designated Airlift Operations officer responsible for his logistics, I felt I couldn't evacuate and leave. If he wasn't coming back to DC, where would he go? What would he need? How would we get it to him? It was my job to figure that out, and I wasn't willing to walk away from that responsibility, no matter what was happening outside.

Colonel Irwin agreed, and with that, he ordered me to quickly grab the Airlift Operations planning binder and to head for the White House basement to the President's Emergency Operations Center—the PEOC—to start coordinating military airlift assets to support the president's movements.

As I reached West Executive Drive, the lush, tree-lined, private road between the Executive Office Building and the West Wing, I could see that both buildings were in full evacuation mode. I was struck by the number of uniformed and plainclothes Secret Service agents with automatic weapons drawn, yelling over megaphones, "Ladies, take off your heels and run for the exits; there's another plane inbound."

Men and women, many of the women barefoot, were streaming out onto the street and sprinting, both right and left, toward the drive's north and south gates—which, although always secured, were now thrown wide open. From the looks on their faces, it was clear the growing crisis had gripped even those working at the very nexus of the country's power center. The anxiety and fear in the air were palpable.

Beyond the gates, the streets were clogged with thousands of workers who had been ordered to leave their buildings and head home. With the Twin Towers ablaze and a huge cloud of billowing black smoke now visible from the Pentagon across the Potomac, most opted not to take the city's sprawling Metro rail system. No one knew where, when, or how another attack would occur. People sensed danger everywhere. We were a city under siege.

Grim-faced Secret Service agents were taking up positions in and around the White House to include the Ellipse to the south and Lafayette Park to the north. I paused for a split second at the surreal sight of the mass exodus before me and then quickly focused on getting to the White House basement. I entered the West Wing under the white awning, flashed my military credentials to the armed agents at the entrance, and bounded down the stairs at nearly a full run.

CHAPTER 7

THE PEOC

Everyone knows, or at least believes, that somewhere beneath the White House, there is a secret chamber of sorts … a hush-hush, nuke-proof room where president's and their most trusted advisors, civilian and military, gather in times of national crisis to observe, from relative safety, cataclysmic events as they unfold.

If you ask the average Washingtonian, particularly those whose offices are within a few blocks of 1600 Pennsylvania Avenue, they will happily speculate (almost conspiratorially) that not only is there such a super safe chamber deep beneath the manicured lawn, but that it has tentacle like hallways and tunnels with exits in buildings many blocks from the White House.

Legends abound about White House tunnels leading to speakeasies during Prohibition, or to hotels where liaisons were arranged. Popular movies, too, have lent an air of computer-generated reality to the notion that such tunnels are pathways to national treasures or international intrigue. However, more mundane, but usually more accurate, accounts detail subterranean White House passageways built in the nineteenth century for water lines and other plumbing structures. Though fanciful stories of below-ground White House escape routes offer an endless supply of fodder for thrillers, what really goes on beneath the Executive

Mansion is sometimes far more interesting—and hair-raising—than fiction.

Depending on who you ask, the chamber might be known as the Tank, the War Room, or the Situation Room. If the person you ask is truly in the know, he or she will make reference to the bunker, or the Presidential Emergency Operations Center—the PEOC, pronounced "pea-ock."

It is from there that the President and his senior staff and military advisors can, if need be, monitor crisis conditions and oversee and direct the men and women who protect our shores and project our power to the far corners of the globe.

The PEOC is manned around the clock by specially chosen military personnel from several services. On the morning of September 11, 2001, I made it to the PEOC from the EEOB—a distance of about two NHL hockey rinks—in record time.

Arriving at the entrance, I picked up the phone, called the duty officer inside, and requested access. The heavy steel door opened. Contrary to what one would think, the PEOC is not particularly spacious. In fact, it resembles a pair of modest corporate boardrooms, but not nearly as plush. "Government issue-plus" is probably the best way to describe it.

The operations section, where the day-to-day staff works, is maybe thirty feet by twenty feet. There's a smaller executive briefing room built off to one side for private conferences. Alcoves fitted with telephones, audio squawk boxes, and television monitors lend a touch of high-energy, state-of-the-art technology. The adjoining executive briefing room has its own designated entrance for the President and his senior staff. Beige walls are trimmed with a dark wood chair railing around the perimeter, adding a touch of elegance, and a low ceiling inset with indirect fluorescent lighting gives the room an intimate feel. Thick blue carpeting throughout completes the decor and helps tamp down even the loudest, most heated conversations.

To the exclusion of everything else, the conference table in the executive briefing room is the PEOC's focal point. It's here, in times of crisis, that the pivotal decisions of high national importance and global magnitude are made. A long rectangle of polished ash, it is big enough to accommodate twenty people seated, with the President or his surrogate sitting halfway down the line of chairs on one side, surrounded by, and facing, his key staff. The presidential seal hangs prominently on the wall behind his chair.

A coffeemaker, cream and sugar, and plenty of cups sit on the neatly set table opposite the chief executive's chair, while notepads and pencils are conspicuously placed within easy reach of everyone at the table. All in all, it is a no-nonsense, no-frills setting that befits the room's sober purpose.

As I entered, I immediately saw a very small contingent of WHMO personnel diligently answering phones and taking notes. No sooner had I announced to the duty officer that I was there to coordinate military airlift assets for the President when I saw my friend, Major Tom Sharpy, one of the vice president's military aides. He was frantically answering phones and giving orders to other personnel.

"Hey, Bob," he yelled, "forget whatever it is you're planning on doing and help me answer the phones. They're ringing off the hook."

I put my Airlift Operations binder down in a corner of the room and immediately grabbed the nearest ringing phone, which turned out to be a direct, secure line between the Situation Room, located in the West Wing of the White House, and the PEOC.

"Major Darling here. Can I help you?"

THE SHOOT-DOWN ORDER OF
UNITED FLIGHT 93

9:52 AM

The call was from the upstairs Situation Room, and the news was heart-stopping. Departing from the businesslike and neutral language used in communications in and around the Executive Office, the staffer on the other end of the line, clearly agitated, just blurted it out: "We have a hijacked plane sixteen miles south of Pittsburgh, inbound to Washington DC."

"Hold on," I answered, attempting to sound as composed and calm as possible, as my military training kicked in to override the enormity of the news. As I turned to pass this information to the military aide, I was startled to see Vice President Dick Cheney, along with the National

Security Advisor, Dr. Condoleezza Rice, standing next to me. The Vice President's wife, Lynn; his Chief of Staff, Scooter Libby; White House Deputy Chief of Staff for Policy, Josh Bolton; and Deputy National Security Advisor, Stephen Hadley, were taking up positions near and behind the Vice President.

"Major, what have you got?" the Vice President asked.

I then responded, "Mr. Vice President, the Situation Room is reporting another hijacked airliner approximately sixteen miles south of Pittsburgh, inbound for Washington DC."

I couldn't help but notice how my corner of the room was filling up fast with White House staffers and other senior advisors. If he was taken aback by the report, the VP didn't show it. The Vice President just turned away to speak into one of the numerous communications speaker boxes now chirping to life above the operations panel. These cutting-edge devices allow two-way, hands-free conversations between the PEOC and outside advisors from any number of federal agencies and the military.

"Rick, are you there?" the Vice President asked. Rick was the federal aviation representative from the FAA's Air Traffic Control System Command Center, or ATCSCC, in Herndon, Virginia, some thirty miles from Washington. "Rick, can you confirm that we have another hijacked plane inbound, approximately sixteen miles south of Pittsburgh, heading our way?"

"Stand by, Mr. Vice President. We're checking."

Within seconds, Rick continued, "Mr. Vice President, they're not talking, they're not squawking their assigned transponder code, and they're well off course. We believe the aircraft is hijacked."

The Vice President turned his attention to another speaker box in an attempt to get Secretary of Defense Donald Rumsfeld on the line.

"Don, are you up?"

"Mr. Vice President, this is the National Military Command Center. How can we help you, sir?"

I knew that the National Military Command Center, or NMCC, at the Pentagon houses the logistical and communications center for the National Command Authority, the principal command and control center of the Department of Defense.

Where the hell is Rumsfeld? I wondered. It was a bit odd to those of us in the military who understood the vital role the National Command Authority plays in times of national crisis that someone as important as the Secretary of Defense wouldn't be at the helm in the NMCC at that particular moment.[1]

As it turned out, the Vice President was unable to reach Secretary Rumsfeld because he was outside on the grounds of the Pentagon, helping the emergency responders tend to the wounded. But the NMCC staff was standing by to take whatever actions were necessary.

Without any hesitation, Cheney ordered, "We have a hijacked plane approximately sixteen miles south of Pittsburgh, inbound to Washington DC. I want two F-15s out of Otis Air National Guard Base. Let me know when they're airborne, and stand by to shoot this plane down!"

From the NMCC came the reply, "Copy all, sir."

I'd been in the room only minutes—and, in fact, still had the phone receiver from my first call in my hand, and I had just witnessed the order given to shoot down one of our own commercial airliners. As unemotional and operationally experienced as two war-zone deployments and fourteen years in the Marine Corps had made me, I still couldn't help but be a little shocked at what I just heard.

I turned slightly to my right to observe the Vice President more closely. I honestly hadn't expected such definitive, lethal action to be ordered so soon, especially from someone other than the President or Secretary of Defense. *This man is no ordinary politician,* I thought. *This man is a warrior!*

The vice president's background had prepared him well for this crisis. He'd been a member of Congress, a White House chief of staff for President Ford, the Secretary of Defense, and now Vice President of the United States. His decades of experience let him see Flight 93 for what it was: no longer a domestic passenger airliner, but the equivalent of a 150-ton Tomahawk cruise missile traveling at more than 500 miles per hour, headed for an unknown target in Washington DC.

While the rest of us were wondering what should be done, he was making the ultimate decision to stop an attack from happening.

---

1 See Afterword

9:58 AM

The NMCC reported back that they had an AWACS aircraft, as well as F-15s, airborne and supersonic over Long Island, New York, and approximately six minutes from the Washington-bound target.

"Please confirm that they are 'weapons free to engage.'" The measured and controlled voice from the NMCC was seeking the ultimate permission to fire on a domestic airliner.

Those of us in the PEOC that day, listening to the NMCC ask for this highest level of permission—knowing that the target was a civilian airliner carrying American citizens—will never forget the heart-stopping implications of that moment ... or Mr. Cheney's reply.

The Vice President did not hesitate. His voice was clear, determined, and free of emotion. "They are weapons free to engage."

10:05 AM

Just seven minutes after the Vice President had cleared the F-15s weapons free to engage, the NMCC riveted the room as it reported over the satellite communications radio, "Aircraft down, aircraft down, approximately sixty miles south of Pittsburgh."

That first report led us to believe that the Air Force, on orders from the Vice President, had executed their mission and taken the draconian measures required to end the impending attack on Washington DC.

Looking back, it was one of many historically grotesque moments of that day. Everyone seemed to freeze. No one spoke. The emotional weight of the transmission seemed to have sucked the air from the room and suspended time. In that deafening quiet, the Vice President slowly turned and looked at all of us as if to contemplate and process what had just happened. He knew what had been demanded of him. He had known what he had to do ... and he had done it.

But he also knew that history was being written—a story unlike any other in America's 225-year democratic experiment. He understood that for posterity, and for the generations of truth-seekers who would forever examine the events surrounding that extraordinary day, he would have to lay down the facts about the interception mission he had ordered our nation's warriors to carry out.

Mr. Cheney walked over to me, looked me in the eye, and said, "Major, for the congressional inquiry, state your full name."

"Major Robert Joseph Darling," I answered crisply.

The Vice President swung around toward the satellite radio on the operations desk and stated, "From Major Robert Joseph Darling to the Vice President to the National Military Command Center, we just shot that plane down."

Mr. Cheney then abruptly announced that he needed to talk with the President, and he walked out. The room was plunged into a thick and heavy silence. Our emotional equilibrium was reeling. There was no doubt in anyone's mind that in the space of ten minutes, we had witnessed a profound, wrenching moment in American history.

10:07 AM

We were again jerked from our private thoughts when the NMCC called back and reported more stunning news in what seemed like the day's never-ending sequence of mind-numbing events.

"The F-15s never fired! The F-15s never fired! The airliner had crashed on its own by the time the fighters got there!"

I can't adequately describe the peculiar sense of elation that overtook everyone at the latest news of what was surely a tragic event. No matter when or where, reports of downed passenger planes always cut to the heart of our worst fears. Yet, in the PEOC that day, the news of the crash brought a confusing mix of inexplicable happiness and soul-wrenching sadness.

I think "relief" best describes it. Despite the horror of knowing that Flight 93 had been doomed from the start, we took real comfort in knowing that America's Air Force—our defenders in the skies—hadn't had to bring down one of our own airliners with our fellow citizens on it.

The Vice President, now back in the room, standing behind me and to my right, said it best when he quietly reflected to no one in particular, "However that airliner crashed, it'll now be remembered as a plane full of heroes, rather than a plane full of victims."

THE COLLAPSE OF THE SOUTH TOWER

10:08 AM

The White House Situation Room called with the news that "CNN is reporting that at 9:59 AM, the South Tower of the World Trade Center collapsed." Since CNN was being monitored in the PEOC, everyone there already knew, and the thought of it was truly incomprehensible.

The Vice President again made it clear that he wanted to talk with the President as soon as possible. He was fidgety and distracted. Striding over to a desk, he barked out, "Does anyone know how many people work in those buildings?"

One of his aides quickly answered, "Mr. Vice President, there are seven buildings in the square, and approximately fifty thousand people work there on any given day."

Momentarily startled at the number, Mr. Cheney turned over a sheet of paper and began furiously calculating the worst-case scenario. Just then, President Bush came on the line. It was the first time that morning we'd heard the President's voice, and there was no mistaking the tenor of the Commander in Chief.

"Dick, what do you have?"

"Mr. President, the South Tower has just collapsed. It's our best guess at this moment that we may have up to twenty thousand dead Americans."

Sounding shocked, agitated, and deeply concerned, the President then asked, "Has anyone spoken to Giuliani?"

"No, Mr. President, we've been unable to reach him."

"What are the hospitals in New York saying? Where's FEMA? What are we doing right now for the people of New York?"

There was a second or two of silence. No one in the room had an answer for the President.

10:11 AM

As the Vice President reached to pick up the handset to take the President off the speaker, the Situation Room called again to report that a section of the Pentagon had just collapsed.

The Vice President, still using the phone's speaker, forwarded the message: "Mr. President, we just got word that a portion of the Pentagon has collapsed. We haven't yet confirmed the casualty figures, but it could be as high as eight hundred to a thousand dead or wounded."

The President seemed to pause momentarily before acknowledging the latest news. And with that, the speaker went silent as the Vice President picked up the handset and he and the President continued their conversation in private.

Seconds later, Major Tom Sharpy, on orders from the Deputy National Security Advisor, called for everyone's attention and announced, "By executive order of the President of the United States, Continuity of Government and Continuity of Presidency programs are now in effect."

By those words, the President had established the defined procedures that made it possible for the government to continue its essential operations during catastrophic events. Key individuals from the executive, legislative, and judicial branches were separated to take up their positions at the now-famous "undisclosed locations." Similarly, he ensured that the executive branch put into effect the established succession plan, should the President and Vice President be killed or unable to fulfill his duties.

On that quiet Indian summer morning, which had started out so deceptively bright and beautiful, it had taken little more than an hour for the nation to reposition itself into full-scale war mode.

ATTACK ON THE WHITE HOUSE

10:13 AM

It was the Situation Room again. This time to relay a message from the Secret Service that a high-speed, low-level aircraft was approximately eight miles out, coming down the Potomac in the direction of the White House.

The Vice President, along with Secretary of Transportation Mineta, turned to the speaker box with the FAA representative on the other end and asked for confirmation that there was an inbound aircraft headed toward the White House.

"We can't see him, sir," was the reply. "He's too low for us to pick up on radar."

The Vice President asked, "Don, are you up?"

For the first time that day, Secretary Rumsfeld responded, "I'm here."

Rumsfeld had just returned from the west side of the Pentagon, doing what he could to help wounded employees who had either streamed out or been carried out from the burning wreckage that had earlier in the day been the south side of the building.

Cheney told Rumsfeld that the Secret Service was tracking an aircraft over the Potomac, heading toward the White House.

"It's eight miles out, coming down the Potomac. Do you have an asset in the air that can take a shot at this guy?"

"We're checking."

I turned to the Vice President with an update. "Mr. Vice President, the aircraft is now six miles out."

Cheney said, "Don, I'll authorize a long-range shot at this guy."

"We're still checking"

I continued my tracking report. "Mr. Vice President, the aircraft is now four miles. Now three miles. The aircraft is—"

The Vice President wheeled around, his face flushed with concern. "Stop!" he commanded me.

The room went quiet. To me, it seemed as if the White House had just succumbed to the inevitable. If the Defense Department didn't have an asset in the Washington area capable of engaging this aircraft—either airborne, as in a fighter, or ground-based, as in a surface-to-air missile—and if there were no Secret Service contingencies in place ready to stop it, there was nothing left for anyone in the room to do except wait for the impact.

I turned and faced my phone console, crossed my hands on the desk in front of me, and thought, *This is going to hurt.*

Many scenarios have been suggested by fiction writers and by military planners about what could be done to stop a determined pilot, flying a fast airplane, from crashing into the White House. The answers to those types of scenarios are, in fact, classified, but we were about to find out in a hurry.

What happened next was surely the best of all outcomes in an otherwise dismal sequence of events. The SATCOM radio blasted to life. "That's not a bogey. That's a MedEvac helicopter heading to the Pentagon!"

As hard as it is to believe, it seemed the hapless pilot had been on the wrong frequency and was apparently not communicating with the control tower at Reagan National Airport. I couldn't help but shake my head. In the worst attack since Pearl Harbor, here was a Medical Evacuation pilot responding to the Pentagon's call for help; and yet, as a result of being on the wrong frequency, at the wrong time, in the wrong place, the entire U.S. military was looking for a weapon with which to kill him. Lucky for all of us, and especially for that pilot, it just wasn't meant to be.

It was one of the few welcome bits of news we heard that day.

10:15 AM

The Vice President and the Secretary of Transportation Mineta were engaged in a private conversation. Secretary Mineta's department included the FAA and, given the still unknown scope of the air attacks, a series of decisions were made to clear American airspace immediately. At the secretary's recommendation, Cheney returned to the room and ordered the FAA to get every civilian airliner on the ground immediately. The FAA's first response was to remind the Vice President that at that moment, there were still more than two thousand airliners in the air coast to coast.

The Vice President said he understood and then reiterated his order: "I want them all on the ground immediately."

10:16 AM

The NMCC announced that at the direction of the President, the North American Aerospace Defense Command (NORAD) had assumed control over all North American airspace, meaning that all aircraft, whether an American Airlines Airbus, a corporate jet, or a Piper Cub at the local flying school, now came under the control of the U.S. Air Force.

This was the first time in our nation's history that NORAD and the United States military had direct control of the entire airspace over North America.

10:17 AM

On the heels of this announcement, the Situation Room relayed unconfirmed reports from the media that a car bomb had exploded at the State Department. This was almost immediately followed by a report of an explosion at the U.S. Capitol.

Rumors were flying fast and furious all around Washington, and phone lines around town were jammed with incoming and outgoing calls assuring worried families and friends that no other bombs had gone off and that loved ones were safe. Communications systems were so overloaded that morning that the cell-phone network across the greater Washington area failed several times in its efforts to keep up with the sheer volume of calls.

The bomb reports caused the attack equation to get even more complicated and dicey. Now the line of thinking was that this attack wasn't just an airborne assault on America, but rather a combined air and ground campaign.

National Security Advisor Rice and others immediately got on the phone lines and tried to confirm or deny these persistent reports, which were adding an element of panic to an already chaotic situation. Within minutes, the initial report was debunked. The reality was that a backup generator had exploded at the State Department, not a car bomb as originally reported. The report of an explosion at the Capitol was also false. In my own mind, these reports highlighted how unsubstantiated rumors could rapidly get out of control and cause growing public hysteria if not checked.

A MOLE ON AIR FORCE ONE?

10:22 AM

I took the call from the Situation Room and immediately turned to Dr. Rice, who was sitting next to me.

"Ma'am, the SitRoom reports that they have a credible source in the Sarasota, Florida, area that claims Angel is the next target."

"Who the hell is Angel?" Dr. Rice asked.

"That's the code word for Air Force One," I replied.

Dr. Rice shot up and ran to find the Vice President to let him know a credible source was claiming that Air Force One was the next target.

"The caller even used the code word, Angel," Rice informed Cheney.

It was yet another piece of unbelievable news on a morning awash in a tsunami of stunning news. The talk among the principals in the room quickly determined that the use of a code word implied that the threat to Air Force One and the President could well be from someone with access to his inner circle—possibly someone who was near the President at that very moment.

The Vice President lost no time in calling the President on Air Force One to fill him in on the latest message traffic. Simultaneously, Major Sharpy called and notified the NMCC that the Vice President was ordering fighter escorts to protect Air Force One from a possible in-air attack. It wasn't lost on anyone in the PEOC that we had gotten word of an unaccounted-for airliner last seen in the Atlanta, Georgia, area headed southeast toward Florida.

"We're getting reports of a threat against you," Cheney told Bush. "It appears credible. We're scrambling fighter escorts, and the Secret Service is taking internal precautions on board Air Force One as well."

The President was immediately placed in his office at the nose of the airplane with armed Secret Service agents at the door, guarding the entrance. Colonel Mark Tillman, Air Force One's pilot, ordered the cockpit door shut and locked with armed agents outside. All press personnel were locked down in the back of the aircraft and ordered to shut down their communication equipment. Air Force One went into full defensive mode as a communications blackout took effect, and the aircraft made evasive maneuvers by accelerating and climbing high above normal airliner-use airspace.

An immediate investigation ensued. The Deputy National Security Advisor, Stephen Hadley, approached me. "Major Darling, what *exactly* was said by the SitRoom personnel about the threat to the President and the use of the code word Angel?"

I went through my notes with him, and he thanked me before moving on to debrief his next subject.

To this day, it has never been determined why either the "credible source" or Situation Room personnel used that code word in their report to the PEOC. What may have started out as a generic threat against Air Force One became a specific threat against the President himself simply because someone in the communications chain, with knowledge of the code word, wrongly placed it into the conversation.

"AUTHORIZED TO ENGAGE ALL INBOUND AIRCRAFT TO WASHINGTON DC."

10:24 AM

Vice President Cheney, visibly agitated over the report involving the threat to the President, ordered the NMCC to inform NORAD they were now "authorized to engage all aircraft inbound to Washington DC."

In acknowledging the order, the NMCC noted that the Navy had a guided missile destroyer off the coast of New York tracking sixty targets. These so-called targets were some of the nearly two thousand airliners that the Vice President had just ten minutes earlier ordered to land immediately. They were being sequenced for landing at the JFK, Newark, and LaGuardia airports.

The cascading series of events over the past hour had begun to take its toll on the Vice President's patience and willingness to leave the country open to yet another attack. He was chillingly clear in his next order to the military.

"I want a firing solution for every one of them. If someone attempts to deviate or does not comply with their landing instructions, I want them shot down!"

STRATEGIC NUCLEAR FORCES TO DEFCON 3

10:26 AM

The President called to convene an air-threat conference. On the call with the President were the Vice President, the Secretary of Defense, and the National Security Advisor.

The Vice President was updating the President on the status of all of the morning's events when Secretary Rumsfeld interrupted, "Mr. President, in my estimation, the quickest and most efficient way to get all of our military forces, worldwide, in a ready condition would be to raise the national defense posture and move our military and strategic nuclear forces to DEFCON 3."

"That's a good idea," answered the President. "Let's move our forces to DEFCON 3. And have them stand by for DEFCON 2."

Dr. Rice's reaction to the upgraded DEFCON status was in keeping with her impressive academic credentials, most notably as a former full professor and provost at Stanford University. She turned to give me a brief history lesson.

"Major Darling, you know the last time we went to DEFCON 2?"

"No, ma'am," I replied.

"It was during the Cuban missile crisis in 1962. And that was only for North America, not worldwide. Now we're going to a worldwide DEFCON 3 status and standing by for DEFCON 2."

The stark import of her words was not lost on me.

As she was explaining, the Vice President interrupted her. "Condi, make it happen."

Without hesitation, Dr. Rice picked up the direct line to the NMCC. "This is the National Security Advisor. By executive order of the President of the United States, move our military and strategic nuclear forces to DEFCON 3 and have them stand by for DEFCON 2."

Chills were running up and down my arms. I couldn't believe I was sitting in the middle of our nation's leaders, listening to them take these decisive actions of global magnitude in order to wrest our country back from terrorists. There was no question in my mind that these were the right decisions to protect America, and I was proud to be among them. I always will be.

Less than a minute after the order was given, the satellite communications radio came to life as, in sequence, each of the military's Unified Combatant Commands acknowledged their orders by crisply reporting:

"This is STRATCOM. We are DEFCON 3, standing by for DEFCON 2."

"This is SOUTHCOM. We are DEFCON 3, standing by for DEFCON 2."

"… PACOM …"

"… CENTCOM …"

"… EUCOM. We are DEFCON 3, standing by for DEFCON 2."

The incoming calls continued until all the combatant commands within the U.S. military acknowledged the new threat level and the possibility of its moving higher. I leaned back in my chair, took a deep breath, and thought, *America is never going to be the same again. I need to call my wife.*

THE UNTHINKABLE HAPPENS

10:28 AM

Suddenly, almost in unison, every eye in the room locked onto the TV. As the unbelievable images seared themselves onto our collective consciousness, some shouted out in anger and rage, and others sat quietly in disbelief. Much like the millions of Americans across the nation who were watching this nightmare unfold, we were shocked at what we were seeing. It seemed almost impossible to grasp that both of the Twin Towers were now on the ground, leaving in their wake a billowing, ash-filled cloud that covered lower Manhattan like a gray shroud.

The President was still on the phone. The Vice President was speaking in a low, matter-of-fact tone. I heard him say, "It could be as high as forty thousand dead." After a few more muffled sentences, Mr.

Cheney slowly put down the receiver and turned to leave the room. I wanted to throw up.

My grief quickly turned to rage. It was time to unleash the full might and power of the U.S. military against our enemies! *The world must know that we won't sit back and be intimidated by any two-bit piece-of-shit terrorist organization. If the world won't confront the problem of radical Islam, the United States will. Soon it will be America's turn, and every f_ing terrorist must die!*

THE RUSSIAN PRESIDENT

10:35 AM

My phone rang and, when I answered, someone in the Situation Room announced, "We have President Putin on the phone for the President. Will you take the call?"

"Whoa, wait a minute," I replied. "You're going to have to hold on."

I turned toward the Vice President and attempted to get his attention. "Mr. Vice ... Excuse me, Mr. Vice Pres ..." But I was making no headway against the many conversations in the room. No one was paying attention to me.

It didn't take me a New York minute to realize I wasn't going to get anywhere by being polite; and so, in a loud Marine Corps commanding voice, I yelled out, "I have President Putin on the phone, holding for the President!"

Needless to say, I got everyone's undivided attention. Almost simultaneously, Vice President Cheney and Dr. Rice turned to me and paused. The Vice President seemed to take a deep breath and then, with a slight drop of his shoulders, turned and quietly said, "Condi, you take the call."

Dr. Rice told the Situation Room to put the Russian President through. Immediately she began speaking in a clear, calm, welcoming tone.

"Mr. President, thank you for the call. And thank you for standing down your forces. President Bush is looking forward to talking with you the first chance he gets. We don't know yet know the full size and scope of these attacks or whether or not they're over."

During the pause that followed, the Russian President was apparently offering his American counterpart condolences and good wishes, because Dr. Rice ended the call by saying, "Thank you, Mr. President, I'll be sure to tell him. Good-bye."

Quite a few of the staff listening nearby wondered what Condi Rice meant by the loaded words, "Thank you for standing down your forces." One of my colleagues in the room suggested that when the United States went DEFCON 3, the Air Force missile crews probably moved the covers off our ICBMs and scared the hell out of the Russians. No wonder Putin had called so fast!

I later learned that there are key individuals within the State Department whose job it is to exchange critical information and notify their counterparts in the former Soviet Union whenever the United States changes its nuclear defense posture. These individuals are part of the Nuclear Risk Reduction Center, an agency created to prevent the mother of all tragedies resulting from some miscommunication between our two heavily armed nuclear nations. On September 11, when the President ordered our nuclear forces to DEFCON 3, the State Department had immediately notified counterparts in Russia about the action that we had taken and presumed that they would, in turn, move their nuclear arsenal to an equivalent state of readiness. But they chose not to. So when President Putin called the White House and Dr. Rice personally thanked him for standing down his forces, she was acknowledging the Russian President's decision not to put his strategic nuclear forces on alert to match our decision to move to DEFCON 3.

It goes without saying that it definitely would have created additional tension in an already explosive situation.

WHERE'S THE SPEAKER OF THE HOUSE?

10:45 AM

Some background may be helpful in understanding what happened next.

According to the continuity of government and continuity of presidency measures, the leadership of our three branches of government—and those in the line of succession to the presidency—are ordered to each move to their individual, predetermined, hardened sites around the country. This better enables them to survive a nuclear attack, for example, or a man-made or natural catastrophic event, and take on the responsibilities to maintain the federal government's operations.

The Speaker of the House is third in the line of succession to the presidency. Should the President and Vice President become incapacitated or die, the House Speaker would be sworn in as the next President of the United States. Clearly, in a national crisis, such as 9/11, it's essential to track and know exactly where each leader is at all times.

It was midmorning when Dr. Rice approached me. "Major, do you know where the Speaker of the House is supposed to be evacuated?"

"Yes, ma'am, I do," I answered.

"Well, he's not there," she replied, sounding a bit irritated. "Can you find out where he is and let me know ASAP?"

"Yes, ma'am."

Over the ensuing few minutes, my Marine Corps leadership training and ability to think fast on my feet helped me work through the national security advisor's problem.

I moved around the room, looking for an available phone and wondering how I was going to contact the unit responsible for moving the Speaker of the House. It wasn't as if I knew the phone number. Abruptly turning around, I was shocked to see Dr. Rice standing right behind me, following me in my circuitous walk around the room.

"Well?" she asked—probably wondering what the hell I was doing.

"Yes, ma'am," I said as I immediately picked up the only phone that was not in use and called the White House switchboard. "This is Major Darling in the PEOC." I asked that they connect me to the commanding officer of the responsible military unit.

The phone rang, and the squadron commanding officer picked up. I briskly introduced myself. "Colonel, I'm calling from the PEOC in the White House. I'm standing here with the National Security Advisor. The Speaker of the House has not yet reported in. Is he where he needs to be?"

"Major, I won't discuss this with you over a non-secure phone."

"Understood, sir. However, there isn't a secure phone available right now." Behind me, Dr. Rice was growing more impatient with each passing second.

"As I said, Major, I won't—"

"Colonel, I'm not asking where you brought him. I just want to know if you delivered him."

Now out of patience, Dr. Rice loudly interrupted me, "Major, I want an answer, and I want it now!" I nodded, turned my attention back to the recalcitrant colonel, and tried to appeal to his sense of rank.

"Sir, I've got important people on this end who need an answer. I only have time for a simple yes or no."

The colonel stubbornly repeated himself. "I cannot give that information out over a non-secure line!"

I was more than annoyed by the colonel's inability to adjust to what was clearly a national crisis. In fact, I had lost my patience with him. And with the National Security Advisor standing next to me, I put all decorum aside as I bluntly told him, "Colonel, at this point, they couldn't give a shit if you yelled it through a Dixie cup! Is the Speaker where he needs to be or not?"

Turning to me, Dr. Rice chuckled and said, "Hang up on that moron." I was more than eager to comply.

Thankfully, at that very moment, the satellite communications radio loudly announced, "The Speaker of the House has arrived; the Speaker of the House has arrived."

The mounting pressure evaporated with those seven words. Clearly as relieved as I was, Dr. Rice graciously thanked me and moved on to her next task.

10:55 AM

The Situation Room reported that all federal buildings had been evacuated, and the Senate leadership and Speaker of the House were now all accounted for.

11:00 AM

With the nation's leadership now in place at their assigned locations, the Vice President and Secretary of Transportation Mineta, along with Dr. Rice and others, busied themselves trying to account for every airliner in the United States. There were reports that NORAD was scrambling jets all over the country, chasing at least ten aircraft that were either not squawking their assigned air-traffic-control codes or not complying with their air-traffic instructions in some way. Some were legitimately requesting priority handling to land due to their low-fuel state or some other type of noncritical emergency.

THE PRESIDENT AND THE MINIVAN

11:45 AM

President Bush arrived at Barksdale Air Force Base, outside Shreveport, Louisiana, to an arrival ceremony that was far from presidential. It was an arrival that gave me particular heartburn, because my original reason for going to the PEOC that morning had been to coordinate the support of the President with the Air Mobility Command. That included the presidential limos, helicopters, phones, and other communication hookups.

But when the President arrived, CNN captured him coming down the steps of Air Force One and, instead of a sleek, reinforced, specially outfitted, top-of-the-line limousine, the Commander in Chief climbed into a waiting and well-used, government-issued blue minivan that had seen better days.

From an Airlift Operations viewpoint, it was a disappointing sight, to say the very least. It looked as if a four-star Air Force general literally had to slide over so the President of the United States could join him in the second row seat for the short ride to the command headquarters.

The men and women of Airlift Operations took great pride in ensuring that all of the comforts of home were waiting for the President, no matter where he went. But getting everything in place prior to an arrival required days of carefully orchestrated planning and cooperation among several services and organizations. No request was too big, no detail too small. On that Tuesday morning, there had been no possible way to outrun the mighty Air Force One and get everything into position ahead of the President.

Watching President Bush climb into a nondescript, commercial minivan was, in truth, a bit of a professional embarrassment for me—something my Airlift Operations colleagues enjoyed ribbing me about. But thankfully, there's an addendum to the story. It was later clarified to us that the President, though he appeared to be climbing in the minivan, had in fact not been placed in the lowly blue minivan that we had seen on TV that day, but had actually been transferred to a nearby armored Humvee for safety reasons. Our reputation in Airlift Operations was still intact!

11:58 AM

The NMCC notified us that Secretary of State Colin Powell, who had been in Lima, Peru, during the attacks, was now airborne and headed back to the States. Given Secretary Powell's position in the line of presidential succession, it was of paramount importance to Airlift Operations that he arrived safe and sound.

As a former four-star general, Chairman of the Joint Chiefs of Staff, and finally, Secretary of State, Colin Powell had the respect and admiration of many in the nation, in the global diplomatic community, and especially among legislators in both houses of Congress. On September 11, had something happened to the President, Vice President, the Speaker of the House, and the President Pro Tempore of the Senate, the Secretary of State may have become next in line to the presidency. The fact that Colin Powell was safely back in the country made many at the highest levels of government breathe a sigh of relief.

According to the U.S. Code, Section 19, the following Cabinet members shall assume the role of acting president in the following order: Secretary of State, Secretary of the Treasury, Secretary of Defense, Attorney General, Secretary of the Interior, Secretary of Agriculture, Secretary of Commerce, Secretary of Labor, Secretary of Health and Human Services, Secretary of Housing and Urban Development, Secretary of Transportation, Secretary of Energy, Secretary of Education, and Secretary of Veterans Affairs.

1:45 PM

The President boarded Air Force One, departed Barksdale Air Force Base, and headed for Offutt Air Force Base, the former home to the Strategic Air Command.

1:46 PM

As a result of the President's earlier order to elevate our military forces to DEFCON 3, the U.S. Navy reported that a Navy battle group had left Norfolk, Virginia. It consisted of two aircraft carriers, the USS *George Washington* and USS *John F. Kennedy*, which were escorted by two frigates and two guided missile destroyers. This armada was ordered to depart port and await further instructions from the Joint Chiefs of Staff.

The deployment of such an enormous armada of warships, in fewer than three hours from the time the President ordered it done, was an incredible feat and a testament to the true professionalism of the U.S. Navy.

THE TWO UFOS

1:57 PM

The Situation Room called to report that they were receiving reports that there was a "high-speed, low-level" aircraft heading in the direction of the President's ranch in Crawford, Texas. I notified the Vice President, who then ordered the NMCC to scramble two F-16s from Kelly Air Force Base in San Antonio, Texas, to intercept it.

At full power, as they traveled past the suspect aircraft at speeds in excess of Mach 1, the F-16 pilots reported in. "The bogey isn't a bad guy or a fast mover—it's just a crop duster."

In true jet-jockey fashion, the F-16 pilots buzzed the much smaller and relatively fragile airplane with such force and speed that they were probably relieved to see that its wings didn't just fold up underneath it in flight. Back at the PEOC, in a rare moment of levity that day, the staff joked that the crop duster's pilot must have landed and immediately called the local sheriff's office to report that he had just seen two UFOs!

2:55 PM

Air Force One arrived at Offutt Air Force Base, where the President entered the command bunker and convened an air threat conference with his National Security Council. It was during that conference that the NMCC reported that a U.S. Airways airliner bound from Madrid, Spain, to Philadelphia, Pennsylvania, was transmitting an emergency transponder code and that the initial reports were that they had a confirmed hostage situation on board.

3:11 PM

The President, Vice President, Secretary of Defense, and others discussed this newest twist in the day's events. They agreed that if the aircraft refused to turn around and continued toward the United States, the moment it got within four hundred miles of our nation's borders, the U.S. Navy would be authorized to use deadly force to bring it down. This report was treated with amazing calm in the PEOC. I think the feeling was that, with three thousand miles of Atlantic Ocean between Spain and the United States, they finally felt they had a situation where adequate time existed to let the crisis on board the aircraft play itself out.

3:30 PM

The next report we received was to advise the Vice President that the airliner had in fact turned around and was returning to Madrid. Apparently, the airliner had not had a hostage situation on board, as first reported, but rather a passenger suffering a heart attack, which had prompted the pilot to squawk the emergency transponder code.

3:35 PM

The President, still at Offutt Air Force Base, discussed with his National Security Council the latest intelligence, the status of the FAA's efforts to clear the skies of all commercial air traffic, and other situational reports from around the country. Based on the information received, the President was to then decide whether he would return to the White House.

THE ESCAT ORDER
AND THE FBI's HOSTAGE RESCUE TEAM

3:50 PM

As a result of NORAD taking control of the skies over North America, no general aviation or commercial aircraft was allowed to fly without the permission of the U.S. military. Under the Code of Federal Regulations, Title 32: National Defense, the Emergency Security Control of Air Traffic (ESCAT) was officially placed into effect. ESCAT provides the procedures to identify and control non-military air traffic within a specified air-defense area during air-defense emergencies. The usual requests to fly during an ESCAT condition come from law enforcement, Flight for Life, or Special-Assignment Air Missions. The Special-Assignment Air Missions are White House-designated missions for essential personnel or equipment as directed at the highest levels of the executive branch. For the White House Military Office, that level of authority comes from the White House deputy chief of staff or above.

With the PEOC in the midst of monitoring an air-threat conference involving the President, Vice President, Secretary of Defense, and others, I overheard Colonel Mike Irwin talking on the phone with a senior member of the Federal Bureau of Investigation (FBI) who was requesting White House airlift support for their Critical Incident Response Group, or CIRG, that was stranded in San Francisco, California, with no way to get back to Washington.

So what? I thought. *There are probably thousands of law-enforcement officers stranded around the country right now who would like to be reunited with their units. What makes this one so important?*

It didn't take long, however, before this specific request was escalated and into the hands of Joe Hagin, the White House Deputy Chief of Staff. And he certainly didn't sit on it for very long. He simply handed it right back to Colonel Irwin and said, "I want you to get these folks back to DC immediately! Let the military know this is a White House priority."

Apparently, the FBI's Critical Incident Response Group is no ordinary federal law-enforcement unit. This is the unit that coordinates the FBI's rapid response to crisis incidents, including terrorist attacks. They also respond to hostage takings, child abductions, and other high-risk repetitive violent crimes. And CIRG is the unit that oversees and operates the FBI's Hostage Rescue Team, the elite counterterrorism tactical team for the United States government. They commonly function as a national SWAT team in highly sensitive or dangerous situations. They are *the* domestic counterterrorism unit, offering a tactical resolution option in hostage and high-risk law-enforcement situations. It made perfect sense that the President would want them home and at the ready, given the day's events.

And with that, the return of CIRG and the FBI Hostage Rescue Team became my number-one mission priority. I had no sooner picked up the phone to begin the necessary coordination with NORAD for a military airlift asset to be sent directly to San Francisco International to bring the FBI Hostage Rescue Team home when the phone at Colonel Irwin's desk rang again. This time, it was a representative from United Airlines, and he wanted to help us.

Because United Airlines Flight 93, which had originally been scheduled to fly from Newark International Airport in New Jersey to San Francisco International in California, had never made it after being hijacked by terrorists (ultimately crashing in Shanksville, Pennsylvania), United Airlines had arranged for grief counselors and other mental-health professionals to be on hand at the United Airlines terminal in San Francisco to assist the grieving families and friends of the passengers from that flight. They also had plenty of pilots and aircrew on hand as well. When the word reached the airline executives that the FBI had essential personnel who were trying to get back to Washington DC, United quickly offered its services. If the White House would authorize the airliner to fly under the White House Special-Assignment Air Mission designator, United Airlines would provide the aircraft and aircrew to get the FBI passengers back to DC immediately.

Because the United Airline pilots and crew were already at the airport and ready to go, this option was both the quickest and the most practical solution. It also freed up the military airlift asset so that it could be used elsewhere. With the Deputy White House Chief of Staff's approval and a simple phone call to NORAD, United Airlines had just become Special-Assignment Air Mission Flight 8811.

Little did anyone know at the time that this airliner would cause the White House and the Secret Service great concern in the coming hours!

FBI Special Agent John (name changed at his request) was a member of the FBI Critical Incident Response Group. His team had arrived in San Francisco on Monday evening, the tenth of September, for a week of SWAT-related field training. On September 11, just before 6:00 AM Pacific time, John had been awakened by a phone call from the FBI Field Office in San Francisco: "Turn on CNN—you're not going to believe this!"

A native New Yorker with many FBI colleagues and close personal friends working in New York, Agent John's first thoughts were, *This can't be real. This is not happening.*

He turned to his FBI colleague and roommate, who jumped up out of bed at the news and said to him, "You're never going to forget this moment for as long as you live. You're never going to forget where you were and who you were with when America was attacked, and here I am stuck in a San Francisco hotel room with you in your underwear!"

Agent John immediately thought of his best friend, the best man at his wedding, who was a New York City Port Authority policeman assigned to the World Trade Towers. "I prayed that he was safe, but I also knew that he worked nights at the World Trade Towers, so he should have been off duty when the planes struck." What John didn't know at the time was that his best friend had changed his work schedule around that day so he could have the evening off to attend a family event. He would learn later the next day that his best friend was, in fact, among the 2,603 innocent civilians missing and presumed killed in the attack on the towers that morning.

Both FBI agents got dressed as quickly as possible and headed out for the San Francisco FBI Field Office, where the Special Agent in Charge (SAC) filled them in on all that had happened and told them to get their team together and get out to the airport. Even though the U.S. airspace was closed to all commercial traffic, he'd do his best to arrange for transportation to get them back to Washington as soon as possible.

They packed their gear and headed for the airport. They were amazed at how eerily quiet the streets had become. At the airport, the only visible activity was the large amount of police manning the terminal buildings with bomb-sniffing dogs and patrolling the airport perimeter for any signs of something out of the ordinary.

A few hours later, word came down that the White House had authorized transportation for them to return to Washington and that a United Airlines aircraft and crew had been approved to fly them across the country. Within the hour, CIRG and the Hostage Rescue Team were airborne and headed toward Washington DC.

4:00 PM

The President, still at STRATCOM, was finishing the air-threat conference and with his top advisors and was now listening to an array of reasons from the Vice President, Dr. Rice, and the Secret Service as to why he shouldn't yet return to Washington. But the Commander in Chief wouldn't be kept away any longer. He promptly thanked them for all for their input, stated he was canceling his executive order for Continuity of Presidency, and assertively stated that he'd be returning to Washington immediately.

4:30 PM

The Vice President and Dr. Rice, realizing the President would be back in DC very soon, prepared the staff for his arrival. The Vice President called for a gathering of all "actionable intelligence," meaning the intelligence community had better have the answers to the President's questions regarding who was responsible for this attack and where the United States could find them, by the time the President arrived back at the White House that evening and called for a gathering of his national security team. White House representatives immediately contacted the National Security Agency (NSA), Central Intelligence Agency (CIA), the FBI, and others, as key personnel were dispatched to "hand carry" the intelligence information back to the White House for inclusion into the *second* president's daily briefing book or PDB.

Over the next several hours, principal Cabinet officials, as well as top law-enforcement and military personnel, arrived at the Executive Mansion to await the arrival of the Commander-in-Chief.

SPEECH WRITING, TEXAS STYLE

4:45 PM

Karen Hughes was one of President Bush's most trusted advisors and longtime friends. The President wanted Mrs. Hughes brought to the White House immediately to begin working on the address he was to deliver to the nation that evening. Dr. Rice got the attention of Major Tom Sharpy and ordered him to find Karen Hughes. He pulled out all the stops to find her using the Secret Service, local police, and assorted others. After an exhaustive search, she was found at FBI headquarters in downtown Washington and brought to the PEOC.

From the moment she entered the room, she immediately made her presence known to all. Walking in, she loudly announced, "I need a computer and a place to work." No amenities, no niceties, just right down to business. No sooner than someone offered her his desk than she began haphazardly scattering his items about and clearing space.

What was so remarkable about watching and listening to her was that Hughes stood as she worked, alternating between writing and shouting out questions, words, and phrases to no one in particular.

"What would he say? What … what would he say? Evil acts or despicable acts?" And, as the answer came to her, she would then yell out, "Yes!" and start keying. It was actually very funny to watch.

What was even more amazing was that as I watched the President's address to the nation that night, I listened to Mr. Bush say the very same words that Karen Hughes had been yelling out loud in the PEOC earlier that afternoon. All in all, with the perspective of time, it was pretty cool to watch the speech-writing process and then the delivery by the President hours later. All of us in the PEOC respected the enormity of the task that Ms. Hughes had before her, and we afforded her every bit of the wide berth she needed to complete her historic mission.

THE COMMANDER IN CHIEF RETURNS HOME

6:45 PM

Having arrived at Andrews Air Force Base shortly after 6:30 PM, the President, onboard Marine One, flew past the still-burning Pentagon and landed on the South Lawn of the White House. He was met at the helicopter by Dr. Rice.

The President entered the PEOC via its executive entrance. The operations and executive sections were divided by a wall with a small, two-foot-by-three-foot dark-glass window embedded in it. From the operations side, staff could see into the executive side, and as the President entered, everyone in the room stood up. Mr. Bush told them to take their seats, and he sat down directly across from the Vice President. Staff, like me, working on the other side of the wall in the operations section, hustled over to the one-way window and peered in to witness this historic moment.

It was a riveting session by any standard.

All eyes were on the President. He'd only been in office for seven and a half months. He'd never been officially tested. Actually, no president since Abraham Lincoln had seen such horrific loss of life in a war on American soil, and no president since James Madison, nearly two hundred years ago, had seen the nation's capital city successfully attacked.

We couldn't help but wonder how he would react to the news that was about to be given. The President would learn that there was very incriminating intelligence that Osama bin Laden was, in fact, responsible for the attacks. He would hear that more than three hundred New York City firefighters and police officers were missing and presumed dead, and that the New York civilian death toll was estimated to be in the thousands. He would also hear that the Pentagon had suffered nearly two hundred fatalities, with countless more burned and wounded, and that the fire damage to the symbol of America's military might was beyond extensive; in fact, it was nearly catastrophic.

As I recount this moment in our history nearly nine years later, it still moves me. I was among a select few to witness the reactions of a new President as he learned the country he had taken an oath to defend had been brutally attacked and heavily damaged by a group of calculating terrorists whose only mission that day was to kill as many Americans as they possibly could. All of this destruction and carnage had been accomplished in the name of a militant, religious ideology whose foundations were based on hate, intolerance, deception, and oppression, and whose one clear goal was to bring America to her knees.

The President looked toward the Vice President and indicated for him to recount the day's events. The President, looking down at his tie, just listened. After the Vice President finished, Dr. Rice began to speak ... and then Secretary of State Powell ... and then Secretary of the Treasury Evans ... and then Secretary of Transportation Mineta ... and then FEMA Director Albaugh ... and so on.

The procedure was that if you had something to say, you were to say it; if not, sit quietly. After each principal finished, all eyes went to the President. I remember thinking, *Come on, Mr. President. We're counting on you.*

The President looked up and paused momentarily as he glanced around the room. He started by saying, "FEMA?"

"Here, Mr. President," answered Director Joe Albaugh.

"Joe, I want you on the next plane out of here to New York. Bring your checkbook with you. I hear it's a mess up there."

"Transportation?" the President said next.

"Here, Mr. President," responded Norman Mineta.

"I want planes, trains, and automobiles up and operating by noon tomorrow. We've got to get this country moving again. When you figure it out, let me know."

The President then looked around the room for a second time, and with all eyes on him and the room in complete silence, he gave his first order as a wartime President: "I want to see my national security team upstairs in five minutes. The rest of you, thanks for coming."

The President stood. Everyone rose, and he strode out of the room.

As I reflect back to that underground contingency Cabinet meeting, I thought President Bush looked and sounded great—confident, determined, and in control. He appeared to truly understand the enormity of the tasks that lay before him. By his own admission at some point during the day, his primary job was now that of Commander-in-Chief of the United States of America. You could see it in his face; he was angered, but he also looked determined to bring a crushing end to those responsible.

I drew great comfort at the thought that al-Qaeda and the Taliban terrorists were about to feel the full might and power of the United States military. America was about to become engaged in a struggle for freedom unlike any other in my lifetime. The President was taking us to war. Now the rest of his Cabinet had better catch up.

GET MY CABINET HOME!

7:30 PM

The President was upstairs in the Oval Office with his national security team, prepping for his nationwide address at eight o'clock. Someone ordered sandwiches for those of us in the PEOC, and we sat down to eat and relax for the first time all day. About halfway through my meal, Deputy White House Chief of Staff Joe Hagin walked in and asked, "Where's that Airlift Ops guy?"

"Here, sir," I called out. Hagin came over and thanked me for all I'd done thus far that day and then added, "Major, the President wants his Cabinet home. We need you to coordinate with NORAD and the Air Force to get them back ASAP, in time for a Cabinet meeting first thing tomorrow morning." He then handed me a small piece of paper with three names on it:

Chairman of the Federal Reserve Alan Greenspan
Secretary of the Treasury Paul O'Neill
Secretary of Veterans Affairs Anthony Principi

As I came to find out, Chairman Greenspan was in Zurich, Switzerland, at a conference, six hours ahead of Washington time. When I was given the mission to get Mr. Greenspan home, it was two in the morning Zurich time.

Mr. Hagin gave me Chairman Greenspan's contact information and left. I looked around the PEOC and wondered who was supposed to call the chairman and tell him about the plan to get him home. However, after asking around and getting no takers, I realized that I owned the task—the whole job, from beginning to end.

In order to pull the multi-pronged operation off, I knew right away that I had to call the Air Force and develop a plan. Scott Air Force Base, in St. Clair County, Illinois, is home to an operations center called the Glass Room. Very similar in structure to the NMCC at the Pentagon, it is manned twenty-four hours a day, seven days a week. With NORAD taking operational control of the skies over North America, anyone planning to launch a military plane on a mission had to work through the Glass Room. I called the White House switchboard and asked them to put me through to Scott Air Force Base.

A duty officer answered, "Glass Room, can I help you?"

"This is Major Darling, calling from the White House. I need to talk to the senior officer in charge."

"Stand by," came the reply.

A few seconds later, an Air Force three-star general identified himself and asked, "Major, how can I help you?"

"General, the President wants the Federal Reserve Chairman and other key Cabinet officials brought home from their overseas locations immediately. I've been tasked with making this happen. I'm going to need your help."

"Major, would it be all right with you if I put my colonel on the phone to help you work this out, or do you and I need to dance all night long?"

I felt the sting of the general's sarcasm. He didn't care where I was calling from; three-star generals don't take taskings from, or conduct planning for, majors. I understood that and simply said, "Yes, sir, that would be fine. Thank you."

The colonel I was assigned to work with was nothing short of terrific. I wish I could remember his name. It took him less than ten minutes to call me back with the plan. The Air Force would launch a plane out of Ramstein Air Base, Germany, within the hour. It would land in Zurich, Switzerland, pick up the chairman, and deliver him to Mildenhall, England.

At that point, the chairman would be transferred to a waiting Air Force KC-10 tanker. He was scheduled to arrive in Washington at 8:00 AM, in time for the President's scheduled Cabinet meeting.

With the planes lined up and in the air, my next mission was to call the chairman. Though it was still the middle of the night in Zurich, I dialed his hotel.

"This is Major Darling calling from the United States. I need to speak with Mr. Greenspan, please." The front desk put me through immediately.

As I was announcing to everyone in the PEOC that the chairman's phone was ringing, he picked up and answered, "Hello?" in what seemed to be a very tired, elderly voice.

"Mr. Chairman," I said, "my name is Major Darling. I'm calling from the White House. The reason I'm calling is to—"

I got no further, because the chairman interrupted me by saying, "You're going to have to hold on, Major," and the phone went down with a loud clunk.

I scanned the room with what must have been a quizzical look on my face. "What's going on?" asked several people standing around.

"I'm not sure yet. The chairman just told me to hold on."

After about two minutes of holding, I muttered to one or two of my colleagues sitting nearby, "I think he fell back to sleep."

Just then, an assistant picked up the phone. "This is Bob. Can I help you?"

"Yes, Bob, you can. The President wants Chairman Greenspan brought back to the United States as soon as possible. He wants to see him first thing tomorrow morning at the Cabinet meeting."

Bob asked me what time the aircraft was going to arrive in Zurich and how many people could go home with him. Recalling my conversations with the colonel in the Glass Room, I said, "I think it's going to be a C-20. There will only be room for the chairman and six others."

At that, Greenspan's aide snapped back, "Negative. There are seventeen of us here. Either we all go home, or no one goes home."

I was impressed. Bob was looking out for his whole team. He probably knew that if the chairman returned home without them, they could be left for days, if not weeks, under the current situation.

"Bob," I said, "I understand and appreciate the fact that you're looking out for your entire party, but President Bush expects to see the chairman in the morning, and the fact remains that there's only room for six others on the plane. Now it's up to you to decide who goes and who stays, but the chairman has to be at the airport and on that plane as soon as possible."

Faced with the reality of the moment, Bob agreed to work with the C-20's limitations and said goodnight. Shortly after, I got word that a C-17 Globemaster aircraft, capable of carrying eighty to a hundred passengers, and not a C-20 Learjet, was on its way to Zurich. So, in the end, I was pleased to call Bob back and tell him the good news; the Air Force had decided to use a C-17 aircraft instead!

When there was no immediate positive response to my announcement, I realized it was still the middle of the night in Zurich, and Bob undoubtedly had no idea what the difference was between a C-20 Lear and a C-17 Globemaster. "That means there will now be plenty of room for entire entourage to return to the States."

He seemed relieved. I asked him to please have everyone at the airport and ready to go the moment the jet arrived. He assured me he would and quickly thanked me and hung up.

One down.

The next Cabinet member on the list was the Secretary of the Treasury, Paul O'Neill. He was in Japan on a fact-finding mission. Unlike Chairman Greenspan, Mr. O'Neill had already received word that he was to return to Washington.

I placed a call to the number I had for him in Japan and told him about the early morning Cabinet meeting. "Mr. Secretary," I explained, "I'm working on the details of your return and will contact you as soon as the plan is established."

"Thanks, Major Darling. As soon as I received word that I was to return to Washington, I called the U.S. embassy here and asked them to help. Could you work out my return with Colonel Morenic, the defense attaché here?"

"Will do, Mr. Secretary." Colonel Morenic was the senior military liaison at our embassy in Japan, and working through him made the task much easier. As soon as I learned of the plan from the Air Force, I simply passed the flight pickup information to the colonel, and he took care of what had to be done with the secretary to make it happen.

Since the Air Force had assets in the Pacific theater, specifically in Japan, this mission was relatively easy to coordinate and execute. Like the federal reserve chairman, Secretary O'Neill would also be transported by a C-17 aircraft. The plane would depart from Iwakuni to Yokota, where it would refuel and pick up the secretary and his entire party. Flying non-stop to Andrews Air Force Base, just outside Washington DC, Secretary O'Neill would also arrive in time to take his name-plated seat at the president's Cabinet table.

Two down.

One of the interesting things about working in Airlift Operations is the speed at which priorities shift. On ordinary days, a small revision in the president's itinerary, the addition of an unexpected VIP to a trip, or a flare-up at an international hot spot can make for turn-on-a-dime changes to highly detailed plans and arrangements.

It was no different on an extraordinary day like September 11, because just as I was about to turn my attention to the Secretary of Veterans Affairs, who was the remaining absent Cabinet official, my priorities were abruptly reshuffled.

EMERGENCY EXTRACTION OF A FORMER PRESIDENT

8:42 PM

When I picked up the ringing phone, the man on the other end identified himself as a Secret Service agent with former President Bill Clinton's detail. He went on to say that Mr. Clinton was currently on vacation and business in Australia.

"I understand. How can I help you, sir?"

"Major Darling, the former president is grounded here in Australia and can't return to the States because of NORAD's restriction on general aviation aircraft."

"Yes, that's right. No commercial planes are flying. Only military missions are authorized at this point."

"That's why I'm calling," pressed the agent. "I'd like your help in getting our aircraft clearance to take off and enter U.S. airspace."

I could not help him with that and told him so. "My priority is to get the president's Cabinet home," I explained, and as professionally as I could, I ended the conversation and hung up.

The agent immediately called back and asked to speak with anyone in the PEOC who outranked me. My boss, Colonel Mike Irwin, was in the room at the time. I called out to him, "Colonel Irwin, sir, I'm transferring a call to you."

The agent retold his story and, again, was disappointed when Colonel Irwin gave him the same negative answer.

"We're sorry we can't help you. We're in the middle of coordinating the return of the president's Cabinet, and all available military assets are being used. Unless the former president is in some kind of danger, we can't assist." After a few more obligatory sentences to put an end to the conversation, Colonel Irwin hung up the phone.

Within minutes, the phone rang a third time, and Irwin answered. This time, the Secret Service agent started the conversation by announcing, "We have a credible threat here in Australia against the former president of the United States. I want him moved, and I want him moved now!"

Colonel Irwin replied, "Yes, understood. Hold, please." With that, he handed the phone over to me. We'd come full circle.

"The former president is now our number-one priority," Irwin said to me. "All necessary and available military assets are to be used to extract him from Australia."

Irwin went on to remind me that under the United States Code, Title 3, Protection of the President, the Secret Service had the right to implement security operations in the defense of a president—or former president, for that matter. And, in this case, if there was a credible threat against Clinton, Colonel Irwin felt they had the right to request military assets for Mr. Clinton's safe return to the United States.

On the phone once again with the Secret Service agent, I took his contact information and told him he'd get a call back with the military airlift plan as soon as possible. After hanging up, I immediately called the Glass Room to relay the newest requirement in the day's turn of events.

Within fifteen minutes, the plan was drawn up and under way. The Air Force launched two C-141s from Guam to Alice Springs,

Australia. Refueling and departing from there, the plane flew into Cairns, Australia, to pick up the former president and take him directly back to Guam. From there, President Clinton was transferred to a waiting KC-10 tanker aircraft, which carried enough fuel to fly him non-stop to Stewart Air National Guard Base in Newburgh, New York. The entire operation, from start to finish, took only twenty hours.

In retrospect, and in all honesty, I never knew if a threat really existed against former President Clinton, or if it was just a ploy to get him home. I guess it really didn't matter. What did matter to all of us in the PEOC was the incredible job the Air Force did to make that emergency extraction happen. What a group of professionals they proved themselves to be once again.

8:55 PM

I turned my attention to the last Cabinet member on my original list: Secretary of Veterans Affairs Anthony Principi. His was perhaps the most convoluted trip of all the Cabinet members.

On September 11, Secretary Principi was in San Diego to address a conference of Veterans Administration employees. Shortly before 6:00 AM, three hours behind New York and Washington DC, he was awakened by a phone call from his Washington office advising him of the attacks. Turning on his television, he took in the stark images of the World Trade Center on fire, smoke billowing into the clear blue morning sky.

A native New Yorker, Principi later said, "I felt my stomach sink as events slowly unfolded on the screen in front of me. My first reaction was, 'Oh, my God, please tell me this isn't happening.'"

He knew every foot of the city and was friends with many of its political leaders and key emergency-response personnel. He was sure that people he knew were probably in the thick of it, though he didn't know then that someone very close to him was working in the heart of the World Trade Center complex.

"I got a call from the FBI," Principi said during an interview for this book, "and was told that they had a car waiting for me. As soon as I could get ready, they took me to a safe location somewhere in San Diego." Principi, along with two staff members, waited in the undisclosed location that morning and well into the afternoon while his staff worked to coordinate the military aircraft asset needed to fly him to Washington.

"Finding a plane was proving problematic, and we were running out of time, given that a flight from the West Coast to Washington was going to take at least five hours," said Principi. "Ironically, I was told the plane they had originally planned for me to use had been diverted to help retrieve former President Clinton from Australia."

It was late afternoon, Pacific time, when the White House got involved and assigned the mission to me. I then called Secretary Principi in San Diego.

"Sir, the Marine Corps has a plane at Miramar Naval Air Station that can take you and your two staff members to Washington, though it might have to make a refueling stop mid-continent. We've located a Marine jet, a C-20, and positioned it at Miramar, ready to depart the moment you're aboard."

Secretary Principi was kept apprised of rescue and recovery efforts going on in New York and the Pentagon as the jet winged its way toward the capital. Halfway across the country, the crew made the decision to land at Whiteman Air Force Base in Missouri for fuel.

Whiteman was home to the highly sophisticated B-2 bomber. The U.S. Air Force B-2 bomber is a low-observable, strategic, long-range, heavy bomber capable of penetrating the most sophisticated air-defense systems. Whiteman also was a perfect mid-continent stop for military flights needing to top off their tanks.

According to Principi, just after the jet landed on Whiteman's twelve-thousand-foot runway, its brakes suffered a major mechanical failure. The plane was essentially grounded, unable to continue on to Washington.

Whiteman's commanding general told Principi that there were no other planes on the base that could get him home, but that they were pulling out all the stops to find something that could transport him back east.

"Eventually, someone found a transport plane," Principi recounted. "I think it was a C-130, but it was going to Dover Air Force Base in Delaware, not Washington."

The airplane was on its way to deliver relief supplies to New York and Washington—medical equipment and blood, among other things.

"I asked if the plane could get us to Andrews Air Force Base, but the answer was no," said Principi. "I was told that Andrews was locked down."

In the early morning hours of September 12, the plane, with its precious cargo of blood and relief supplies, touched down at Dover. A government car was waiting to rush the veterans affairs secretary to Washington, but the secretary would not leave immediately. Instead, he and his staff helped unload the supplies first, making certain that the containers were moved quickly from the cargo hold onto trucks ready to make their way to New York City hospitals.

Only after all the supplies were off-loaded did Principi get into his car for the three-hour trip to Washington. The respect he gained from the U. S. military members, as word spread through our ranks of his willingness to stop just long enough to lend a helping hand on that rope line that morning for others in need, solidified to all of us that we had the right man at the helm of veterans affairs.

What Secretary Principi did not know at the time was that his nephew, Vincent Princiotta, a New York City firefighter trying to rescue trapped office workers, had died in the collapse of one of the World Trade Center towers.

"He was a wonderful young man," remembered Principi, "with movie-star looks and a great sense of humor."

The PEOC's efforts to get Secretary Principi home and to the White House were mirrored in all of the Airlift Operations labors that day. Whether we were bringing executives back to Washington from Switzerland or California, we managed to fulfill our assignments and ensure that the President had his full team of advisors at the Cabinet table during one of the most trying times in our nation's history.

WAKE THE PRESIDENT!

11:50 PM

Eight hours earlier, the White House had approved a Special-Assignment Air Mission for United Flight 8811 to carry the seventy-five members of the FBI's Critical Incident Response Group back to Washington Reagan National Airport. With the skies over the United States empty to all commercial traffic, United Flight 8811 was all alone except for the two fully armed F-16 fighter aircraft following close behind.

When the aircraft hit light turbulence, the captain contacted the military command and control aircraft, flying high overhead, to request a change in altitude in search of smoother air. The reply: "You can choose any altitude you want; you're the only commercial up here tonight."

As the airliner and the F-16s sped toward Washington's Reagan National Airport, apparently someone forgot to coordinate with the Secret Service that this plane that was approaching at a high rate of speed was in fact an authorized Special-Assignment Air Mission. When the White House alarms began sounding, indicating an unidentified high-speed aircraft was approaching the Executive Mansion, Secret Service protocol required them to quickly, without hesitation or permission of the first family, enter the president's second-floor residence and awaken the President and First Lady and physically move them down to the White House bunker.

I was working at my console, tracking the progress of the military flights carrying the two Cabinet officials, the Chairman of the Federal Reserve, and the former president of the United States when the Secret Service rushed into the space with the President and First Lady in tow, wearing only their pajamas and carrying their Scottish terrier, Barney.

I glanced over at the President and could immediately tell he wasn't there to see how we were doing. As one might expect, he was very annoyed for having been awakened and physically removed from his bed simply due to a failure in coordination between the military and the Secret Service. As soon as the all-clear was announced, they quickly turned and returned to the residence.

By the look on his face, I hoped for everyone's sake there wouldn't be any more false alarms involving the President that night.

CHAPTER 8

THE AFTERMATH: SEPTEMBER 12, 2001

HOME TO MY FAMILY

9:45 AM

Early the next morning, after a long, sleepless night in the PEOC, I learned that Chairman Greenspan's aircraft had touched down at Andrews Air Force Base. All members of the president's Cabinet were now home. Former President Clinton was airborne and would land at Stewart Airport in New York within hours. A sense of relief washed over me knowing that my mission was coming to an end and that I would soon be relieved by a new White House military officer. I took advantage of the quiet moment to review my notes from the previous day's events and muse over what I knew I would look back on as a defining moment in my life.

White House Deputy Chief of Staff Joe Hagin came over and thanked me for my work over the last twenty-four hours. "Major, on behalf of the President, Chief of Staff, and myself, you did a great job for us yesterday; you're now free to go. Thanks again for everything."

I thanked him, quickly packed my gear, and left.

My new mission was to get home to my family. Although I knew that my wife, Angela, and my two sons Michael and Matthew, were safe, I also knew I needed to see them. After more than twenty-four hours cloistered underground, my drive down the expanse of I-95 South was no less surreal than my time in the PEOC. As anyone who lives in a large metropolitan area like Washington knows, weekday mornings on the road are problematic at best. Traffic is everywhere, and traveling the shortest distances can be measured by the hour. Yet on this particular Wednesday morning, there were only a handful of cars to be seen. It was eerily quiet and empty.

As I drove past the Pentagon, I saw that a few emergency vehicles and personnel remained on its south grounds and in vast parking lots. The huge, blackened gash that spanned almost half of one side of the building was still smoldering from the enormous holocaust of the day before.

My head was reeling from the past twenty-four hours. I couldn't stop my brain from going over and over the momentous events of the day that had just passed—both the horrible tragedies that had occurred and the calamities we had anticipated that had, in fact, not happened.

There had been a lot of information thrown at us, and a lot of misinformation as well—like the fact that for a few brief moments, we all believed that we had shot down United Flight 93, and at one point, we thought we had suffered car-bomb explosions at the Capitol and at the State Department. Thankfully, neither turned out to be true.

And then there was the unbelievable moment involving the Medical Evacuation helicopter that our country was on the verge of shooting down, thinking it was a bogey aircraft attacking the White House. I wondered if the pilot of that helicopter would ever know how lucky he was. Finally, I thought about the shock at the beginning of the day—the mysterious aircraft that had flown over the White House that morning. We had initially believed it was American Airlines Flight 77, passing overhead just minutes before it struck the Pentagon. However, after reviewing my notes for this book and talking with former Secret Service colleagues who were at the White House with me that day, and later interviewing other well-placed military officers at the Pentagon, I learned that it wasn't Flight 77 after all.

The flight path of American Airlines Flight 77 had it approaching Washington DC at a high rate of speed out of the west. When it reached a position four miles west of the Pentagon, it began a right-descending 330-degree turn. It rolled out wings level at approximately 3.5 miles west, southwest of the Pentagon, and then dived and accelerated into the western side of the building. The aircraft that overflew the White House that day was actually an unmarked, militarized version of the 747-200, an Air Force E-4B aircraft that serves as the National Airborne Operations Center for the National Command Authority, including the President of the United States, the Secretary of Defense, Chairman of the Joint Chiefs, and the designated successors. The E-4Bs are often referred to as the "doomsday planes" and are operated by the First Airborne Command and Control Squadron located at Offutt Air Force Base, near Omaha, Nebraska.

Why it was over the White House at that time on that ominous day, I have no idea. And it's likely that we may never know, due to the highly classified nature of its missions.

Looking at the scope of the Pentagon wreckage from my car window, I could easily imagine how the impact of American Airlines Flight 77 must have truly shaken our nation's military command center to its very foundations.

I thought back to the preceding day's stunning news of the attack on the Pentagon and then Angela's call, and I realized that I had never found out whether Christine had located her husband, Tom, at the Pentagon.

Was he all right? Had he survived?

Then I thought about the two women, two anonymous women I'd picked up in the slug line the day before and dropped off at the Pentagon. Had they turned into survivors or victims? I tried to picture them but couldn't. There are so many people we see but don't see in our daily lives. I hoped they were okay.

And what about all the employees I'd watched rushing into the Pentagon to work in that glistening, bright morning sunshine the day before? Had they gotten out or ended up on the casualty lists?

I thought about others—our friends and neighbors and family members who work in New York City.

I really needed to get home.

With no traffic, the drive down I-95 was fast. I pulled into our driveway, jumped out of the car, and ran inside the house. As I came into the foyer and looked around for my wife, I called out to her, "Angela!"

"Bobby!" she shouted from upstairs as she hurried down into my arms. Angela and I hugged. I held her as tight as I could. Neither one of us spoke. We just continued holding on to each other as if our closeness could erase all that had happened. She pulled my face away from hers and looked into my eyes. "Are you all right?"

"Yes, I'm fine. I've missed you and the boys very much, but I have so much to tell you."

CHAPTER 9

ANGELA'S STORY

To tell the truth, I was surprised that Bob came home that next day. After he'd called me late in the morning on the eleventh to let me know that he didn't evacuate but rather was still working "in the safest location of the White House," I was relieved but figured that given the enormity of the events, he wouldn't be home for a while. It was okay, though; as a military wife, I was used to both long and short deployments.

Along with the rest of the country, I'd spent the last twenty-four hours watching the news channels broadcast live reports from downtown Manhattan and then replay the disturbing images—the second plane careening into the South Tower ... the gigantic wall of ash billowing through the canyons of lower Manhattan ... the heartbreaking search and rescue efforts ... and the scenes of the burning wreckages at the Pentagon and in Pennsylvania. It was tragic and surreal.

I first heard about the crash into the first tower on the car radio while on my way to meet my friend Christine at a local coffee shop sometime before 9:00 AM. I called Bob at work to see if he heard about the plane accident at the WTC; he was already watching the news at the office. Christine and I had plans to do some errands and shopping together while our kids were at morning preschool. Together we listened and followed the news happening in NYC with awe and disbelief. Then fear set in once we heard about the crash of another airliner into the side of the Pentagon. Christine's husband, Tom, an Air Force officer, worked at the Pentagon, and she couldn't get through to him on her cell phone. I immediately called Bob to see if he had any information that would assure us that Tom was okay. I could hear the adrenalin in Bob's voice and could tell that he was very busy and needed to get off the phone. I think back now, that in the midst of an unfolding crisis, he still took the time to answer my phone call. Unfortunately, he didn't have any comforting information for us, so Christine and I quickly decided we needed to put our shopping plans aside and get home so we could watch the news.

I was devastated and distraught by the events and images streaming on the television. I was a native New Yorker and felt my own personal connection with the World Trade Centers. I worked in Manhattan for two years and I passed the Twin Towers each morning while commuting to the Lower East Side from my hometown of New City. I couldn't believe they were gone. Years before, I attended my cousin's wedding reception at the renowned Windows on the World restaurant at the top floor of the North Tower. Who did this? How could this have happened?

Like millions of Americans I was glued to the news coverage that day but I was also a mom with two young boys. I couldn't let them see those disturbing images. Michael and Matthew were only seven and four years old and I needed to shield them from the pure evil that caused such loss and devastation.

And although I was happy when Bob came home to us the next day, I was really surprised his job was finished and that he had been allowed to leave his post at the White House. I remember asking, "Is it all really over? Is America really safe now? Are things really back to normal?" In the wake of the attacks and the awful uncertainty that followed, these questions were repeated over and over in my mind, as I'm sure they were in the minds of all Americans.

I greeted him at the front door as he came in the house. He looked a bit tired—unshaven and wearing the same suit he wore to work the day before, but he also looked alert, motivated and eager to talk—he was still in work mode. We walked into the kitchen and stood around the cooking island as he began to relate what had happened, who he was with, what was said, and what he did.

The following hours flowed as if a bottle of champagne had suddenly been uncorked and streams of accounts, anecdotes, and stories spilled out. As he went on, I became in awe of him. He was both a witness and a participant in what must certainly go down as one of the most infamous days in our history. The one thing I really wanted to know was if what I had been hearing on the news matched up to what had *really* happened during those twenty-four hours inside our nation's political nerve center.

Then he started talking about United Flight 93. I started to get apprehensive, because I'd heard the rumors. I could sense he was about to tell me that the order had been given to shoot it down, to blow it out of the sky. All I could think about was how horrible—no, how nightmarish—the last hours of the forty American souls on that plane must have been. I started to feel sick to my stomach. I just couldn't believe it; to me, it was just unthinkable. I wanted him to stop talking. I didn't want to hear him say the words I knew he was going to say. And, if it was true, I didn't want him to ever speak of it or admit it—ever.

Like so many others, I had heard the rumor that the military had shot the airliner down, but I had immediately put that hearsay out of the realm of possibility. It was impossible that the American government would ever do that to its own citizens. In fact, I had even defended the President and Vice President when one of my friends that morning said she heard it was true. I told her, "There is no way that could ever be true." And yet, right in front of me was my own husband, getting ready to tell me that not only was it true, but that he had played a part in it.

I got upset—very upset. I started crying and waving my arm at him to stop talking. I could see by the look on his face that he was in his military work mode; he was telling me the story as if it were just another assignment, another military operation.

I yelled out, "Stop!" He looked down at me and seemed surprised that I was so stricken by what he was saying. I kept repeating, "I can't believe you would say that! Why are you telling me this? Why did you do it?"

In the heat of the moment, Bob realized the staggering emotional toll that singular event had had on me. As he saw how it was affecting me, he got a little choked up himself and said, "You didn't let me finish.

You didn't let me finish. We didn't shoot that plane down! I promise you that we did *not* shoot that plane down!"

I think it was at that highly charged moment that Bob started to decompress emotionally and come to terms with the magnitude of all he had been through. We both took a break and decided to stop talking about it for a while. Like the nation itself, we needed to recover from the shock and sorrow that had us tightly in their grip. After I had been reassured that Flight 93 hadn't been shot down, but had come down at the hands of terrorists, I was able to listen to the rest of his remarkable story. I was so proud of him and all that he had done to serve and support our country and its leaders on that awful day.

The tragedy was especially hard on both of us because we were connected to it on multiple levels. Thankfully, Christine did finally receive a call from Tom that he was all right but we had other neighbors and friends who were either federal employees or fellow military families who were grieving over the loss of their friends and colleagues at the Pentagon.

Our alma mater, Iona College, suffered the loss of fifteen of its alumni, some of which were employees of Cantor Fitzgerald, a global financial services firm, who lost 658 of its employees that day working on the top floors of the North Tower. And I later learned that Bob's cousin's husband, Tom, had actually been in one of the towers that morning and escaped just minutes before it collapsed.

We were so affected by the tragedy and so drawn to it, that in November 2001, Bob and I cancelled our ten year wedding anniversary trip to Hawaii and instead made plans to go to NYC to visit Ground Zero. We both needed to be there. As we walked along the broken streets and sidewalks toward the site we could still smell the effects of the burning debris from the Towers and were overwhelmed with the thousands of pictures, stuffed animals, and flowers left in memory of those killed or in support of our first responders and each other. We stopped to write our thoughts on one of the memorial banners as well. It's something we will never forget.

I think everyone has a 9/11 story. Everyone who can remember it knows exactly where they were and what they were doing on the day that changed America. This was just one of those stories— a Marine's story. It was the story of my Marine, who answered the call to national service and who never once wavered in his love of, and commitment to, our country's highest principles and ideals.

He and his colleagues in all branches of the military have always been proud to face, head-on, the challenges of defending America. Of course, I am particularly proud of the way Bob rose to the many challenges facing him on that terrible day. And I am tremendously grateful he came home safely to the family, community, and nation he pledged to protect so many years ago, on the deck of USS *Intrepid*, in the shadows of the Twin Towers.

CHAPTER 10

CONCLUSION

In the months and years following 9/11, I've watched with pride as America's servicemen and women—wearing the uniforms of the Army, Navy, Air Force, Marine Corps, and Coast Guard—have stepped forward to be counted as warriors in democracy's defense.

As of this writing, more than fifty-two hundred of our finest sons and daughters have given their lives in the defense of our nation, with another thirty-eight thousand service members wounded, in our continuing mission to seek out those who did us harm in 2001 and those who continue to wish us harm.

I drive by the Pentagon often, and I never forget to thank God for what it stands for: the power and might of the greatest nation on earth. The ground at American Flight 77's site of impact is consecrated soil now. The memorial erected there is a mute, but elegant, testament to the sacrifice of the 184 men and women on board the plane and in the Pentagon. As I pass by its outer walls, I remember them all, and I silently promise them I will never forget their sacrifice.

I think of the heroes of United Airlines Flight 93, who would not let the terrorists win, and who may have saved unknown numbers of lives in the nation's capital with their selfless, spontaneous, and collaborative acts of bravery. I hope I would have that much courage if faced with the same decision.

And I think of all our fellow countrymen and citizens of foreign nations who perished in the World Trade Center and the first responders—the firefighters, police officers, New York City Transit workers, and just plain ordinary citizens—who braved a fiery hell itself to save others after American Airlines Flight 11 and United Flight 175 were plunged into the North and South Towers.

As a Marine commissioned on a more innocent morning of our history, I am proud to have played even a small role in the events of that transformational September day. What I experienced in the Operations Center was the same strength of character and strength of purpose that I saw in my friends Tim Sullivan and John McGyver at Iona College; the same commitment to success I shared with my OCS classmates at Quantico; the same unflappable dedication to his brothers in arms that I saw in Kid as he hauled those pallets in place to save the lives of our buddies Box and Irish; and the same love of country that I saw in Angela's eyes as we mourned together over the tragic loss of our fellow citizens and the horrendous disfigurement of our beloved New York City skyline.

Time has a terrible habit of dulling memory, of softening the images of our past, and of placing a darkening glass between us and events in our ever-receding history. As one who witnessed history in all its ageless indifference, I believe we must not let the stark, brutal, and painful images of September 11, 2001, fade into the mists of a thousand yesterdays because we are distracted or diverted by other immediate, more urgent priorities.

In these dangerous and turbulent times, it would do us well to study and examine the past if we are to ensure our future. The nineteenth-century Spanish-born American poet and philosopher George Santayana probably said it best when he wrote these prophetic words more than a century ago: "Those who cannot remember the past are condemned to repeat it."[2]

In memory of the almost three thousand Americans who died that day, and the thousands of others injured, we, the men and women of the United States military, vow to remain vigilant and to protect and defend our way of life against all enemies.

In their names, we will remember.

---

2 George Santayana, *Life of Reason: Reason in Common Sense* (Scribner, 1905), 284.

AFTERWORD

SO WHERE WAS THE
NATIONAL COMMAND AUTHORITY?

The term National Command Authority refers to the President of the United States and the Secretary of Defense. They are the senior lawful source of military orders to the United States military. No *offensive,* lethal military action will ever be taken by any component of the U.S. military without the direct consent of the President or the Secretary of Defense. We all know that on September 11, 2001, the President was at the elementary school in Sarasota, Florida, or on Air Force One, suffering from intermittent communications with his Vice President and National Security Advisor at the White House.

But where was his Secretary of Defense, and why wasn't he in touch with the President that morning? According to his own testimony to the 9/11 Commission, Donald Rumsfeld literally didn't speak to the President until sometime after 10:00 am. In the worst attack on American soil since Pearl Harbor, taking nearly three thousand American lives, destroying billions of dollars' worth of property, sending Americans running in fear through our country's streets, and nearly crippling the world's largest financial system, no official National Command Authority response came until after the attacks had ended. Had it not been for the Vice President interjecting himself into the national military command and control system by ordering our alert F-15 fighters to take offensive lethal action against United Flight 93, ordering the F-16s to protect Air Force One, and ordering other fighter aircraft to establish a Combat Air Patrol over our nation's capital, our country would have been without an official response from both the National Command Authority as well as the entire executive branch of our government.

To add to this dilemma, due to poor communication between the FAA and the pilots from Langley Air Force Base, Virginia, the alert F-16s that were supposed to be over Baltimore, Maryland, establishing a blocking position to intercept the phantom American Airlines Flight 11, when it was thought to be headed toward Washington, were actually hundreds of miles away, over the Atlantic Ocean, in a holding pattern, awaiting further orders.

So the question remains: where was Secretary of Defense Rumsfeld, and why wasn't he at the helm in the Pentagon's National Military Command Center when all of this was unfolding? Could he have made a difference? What information would he have learned? What orders might he have given? Could there have been a better outcome?

According to Matthew Everett, an *Online Journal* contributing writer who wrote an article titled "Donald Rumsfeld on 9/11: 'An Enemy Within,'" the Secretary of Defense was derelict in his duties as a member of the National Command Authority.

Here are just a few excerpts from his article:

> "The Secretary of Defense, by his own account to the 9/11 Commission, deserted his post during the most devastating attack ever to take place on U.S. soil."

According to Everett, even though Secretary Rumsfeld had been informed of the unfolding attack on New York City and Washington, Rumsfeld inexplicably chose to go about his daily routine.

> "The Secretary of Defense started the day with a meeting with members of Congress at 8:00 AM, and then, in spite of being informed of the first attack on the World Trade Center Towers, decided to continue with a pre-scheduled CIA briefing, which lasted quite some time. When the second plane hit the World Trade Center at 9:03 AM, Pentagon officials Torie Clarke and Larry DiRita headed to Rumsfeld's office to discuss what

was happening. At that very moment, the Pentagon's Executive Support Center (ESC) was beginning to swing into action. The ESC is made up of several secure conference rooms, located close to Rumsfeld's office, and is where the Pentagon leadership goes to coordinate military operations during a national emergency. It remains a mystery as to why Secretary Rumsfeld did not go to either the ESC or to the NMCC, which is located next to the ESC, at this critical moment. When Clarke and DiRita arrived in his office, Rumsfeld told them that, instead of going to the command center, he wanted to continue with the CIA briefing and make a few phone calls.

"At 9:37 AM, when Rumsfeld was in his office with the CIA briefer and heard the terrific boom of the impact of American Flight 77 on the building, he again did not report for duty and take the helm of the NMCC as he should have, but rather ran outside to the Pentagon parking lot to help with moving the wounded on stretchers. This is remarkable, especially considering that no one at that time knew how many attacks were still pending. The fact that Rumsfeld was missing from his office at the Pentagon created tremendous confusion for the next twenty minutes or so, as officials were frantically trying to locate him.

"All of this makes clear that, as a key member of the National Command Authority, Secretary Rumsfeld not only broke the chain of command but abandoned his post on 9/11. Rumsfeld did not enter the ESC until 10:15 AM and the NMCC until 10:30 AM, which was well after the time he could have made a difference."

WOULD SECRETARY RUMSFELD'S PRESENCE IN THE NMCC HAVE MADE A DIFFERENCE?

Let us assume, for the sake of argument, that Secretary Rumsfeld had, in fact, responded to the National Military Command Center at 9:03 AM, immediately after the second airliner, United Airlines Flight 175, impacted the South Tower of the World Trade Center. It was at that moment that it became crystal clear, at least for the rest of America and the entire world watching the news that morning, that New York City was under direct attack by terrorists using commercial aircraft as weapons of war. What would have changed? What actions might he have taken?

At approximately 9:04 AM, the moment he would have stepped through the door and asked, "What's going on, and what do we know?" this is potentially some of the information he may have been told.

The secretary would have learned that at 8:46 AM, as a result of the North Tower attack, two F-15 alert aircraft located from Otis Air Force Base in Falmouth, Massachusetts, had been ordered to battle stations and were currently airborne and holding over Long Island, New York, awaiting further instructions.

The secretary would have also learned that the North Tower was struck by American Airlines Flight 11 and the South Tower by United Airlines Flight 175, and that both hijacked aircraft had originated out of Logan Airport in Boston.

Five minutes later, at around 9:09 AM, the secretary would have been notified that the North East Air Defense Sector (NEADS) Commander, in consultation with the FAA, was now vectoring the F-15 aircraft over Manhattan from Long Island and that the alert F-16 aircraft from Langley Air Force Base, Virginia, were being placed to battle stations awaiting further instructions.

Over the next twenty minutes, the secretary would have most likely attempted to consult with the FAA and military command and control leadership and quickly learned that both were incredibly overwhelmed. He would have then received an erroneous report that American Airlines Flight 11 was not the aircraft that crashed into the North Tower in New York and in fact may still be airborne and heading toward Washington DC.

The NEADS Commander would have then informed him that the Langley alert F-16 fighters were now scrambled and airborne and being vectored to Baltimore, Maryland, to position themselves as a blocking force to react to American Airlines Flight 11 the moment it reappeared on radar.

It was at this specific moment that the Secretary of Defense would have surely interjected himself into the process as the clear authority regarding the Rules of Engagement (ROE) for those F-16 pilots. His presence on the communication net would have definitely gotten the attention of General Ralph Eberhart, the NORAD Commander, who would have ensured the orders of the Secretary of Defense were clearly understood by his pilots and followed to the letter. This action alone would have certainly put more focus on the importance of those F-16s' being over Baltimore, Maryland, ready to intercept the incoming terrorists, rather than vectored eastbound somewhere over the Atlantic Ocean, hundreds of miles away from Washington DC. The secretary also would have wanted to contact President Bush to confirm, officially, that the President had in fact authorized shoot-down orders for our fighter pilots.

At 9:20 AM, the secretary would have also learned that the FAA at Indianapolis Center was now also looking for American Airlines Flight 77 and that its previous assumption that it had probably crashed was incorrect, and that they now feared that it, too, had been hijacked.

At 9:32 AM, when American Flight 77 suddenly reappeared on radar to the Dulles controller to be coming out of the west at a high rate of speed toward Washington DC, the secretary would have most likely authorized the Langley F-16 fighters, now just forty miles away, over Baltimore, Maryland, to attack and engage the incoming hijacked airliner as quickly as possible. Given the incredible capability of the F-16 aircraft, they just might have had enough time to intercept it. At more than 500 miles per hour, the hijacked airliner could travel its last six miles to the Pentagon in less than a minute. However, as was previously described, American Flight 77 didn't fly directly to the Pentagon. When it was approximately 3.5 miles west of the Pentagon, it suddenly began to descend and turn hard to the right. It continued its turning descent until it leveled off at two thousand feet in altitude and was again pointed at the Pentagon. Over the next thirty seconds, it pitched its nose down, accelerated to more than 530 miles per hour, and crashed into the west side of the Pentagon at 9:37:45 AM.

Had the F-16s been given the order to attack American Flight 77 at 9:32 AM, it would have taken them less than a minute to move within weapons-release parameters and even less time for their AIM-120 Advanced Medium-Range Air-to-Air Missiles, known as AMRAAM missiles, traveling at over Mach 4, to find their target. The fact is that on 9/11, they would have had a full five minutes, more than enough time to find that aircraft, engage it, and destroy it before it hit the Pentagon at 9:37 AM.

With the destruction of American Airlines Flight 77 somewhere over Washington and the threat of the phantom American Airlines Flight 11 still looming, the secretary would have most likely ordered more fighter aircraft to the Washington DC area. At 9:52 AM, when the PEOC received word that United Flight 93 was hijacked, sixteen miles south of Pittsburgh, Pennsylvania, and inbound to Washington DC, there would have been numerous armed fighters either in position or rapidly moving into position to engage the terrorists in that aircraft. Had the passengers not ended the mission of those terrorists at 10:03 AM, the military surely would have.

SECOND-GUESSING

Although I too, believe Secretary Rumsfeld's appointed place of duty was at the helm in the NMCC that day, there's no indication that any of these hypothetical scenarios I proposed would have changed the devastating outcome for the better. If the secretary had been successful in intercepting and shooting down American Airlines Flight 77 somewhere over Washington DC, he might have saved the lives of those in the Pentagon only to doom countless others who might have been caught in the fiery debris as the aircraft came down on top of them.

The same could be said for the passengers on board United Flight 93. Instead of crashing in a vacant field in Shanksville, Pennsylvania, the plane may have been shot down over a heavily populated town or urban center, potentially killing scores of innocent people on the ground. And let us not forget about the MedEvac helicopter that was initially reported to be an unidentified, high-speed, low-level aircraft coming down the Potomac, headed for the White House. There is a real possibility that it, too, would have been blown from the sky somewhere over Washington DC if we had the fighters in the area that could have engaged it.

The real questions still remain; why did Secretary Rumsfeld abandon his post that day by not responding to the National Military Command Center the moment the attack on our country was realized? Why didn't he attempt to contact the President sooner? Why was the National Command Authority so ineffective? Can America count on that type of command and control structure to protect us in the future?

This current system of command and control, which places so much of our military response authority in national emergencies in the hands of just two people—one who could not communicate well due to technological reasons and the other who simply chose not to, failed to protect us from our enemies on September 11th and revealed tremendous flaws in the National Command Authority structure. Surely America can and must do better if we are to prevent similar tragedies from happening in the future.

In spite of that key failure, our country did respond well, thanks to the actions of so many from all aspects of American life, including the tough decisions made by the Vice President in the PEOC; the leadership of Colonel Robert Marr, the NEADS Commander; the military pilots who were willing to push the envelope to protect us; the many determined FAA controllers who would not give up trying to make sense out of unbelievable chaos; the thousands of brave and competent airline pilots who cleared the skies without a single aircraft or ground taxi mishap; our heroic first responders; and of course the incredible Americans onboard Flight 93 who fought and thwarted the terrorists from succeeding in their mission. Thank you all for your courage.

MOVING FORWARD

After 9/11, the Bush administration did initiate enormous, positive steps toward improving the security of our nation. In a major organizational addition to the Department of Defense, Congress approved the creation of a new combatant command known as NORTHCOM, or Northern

Command, on October 1, 2002. This new command now works in concert with the North American Aerospace Defense Command, or NORAD, and falls under the command of a single four-star general. According to Air Force General Victor Renuart, the current commander of both NORAD and NORTHCOM, in his testimony to the Senate Armed Services Committee, he described the two commands as now being "inextricably linked" in their missions to defend America. While NORAD will continue to search for threats coming from over the horizon and from space, NORTHCOM's mission will be to protect the United States homeland and support local, state, and federal authorities.

Additionally, NORAD is now plugged directly in to the Domestic Events Network (DEN). The DEN is described as a nationwide, open phone line, managed by the FAA, that was designed to provide open and improved communications for federal agencies with jurisdiction over the security of the U.S. airspace. The agencies that now participate in the DEN include the Transportation Security Administration, Department of Defense, FAA and FAA Field Offices, National Capitol Police, Immigration and Customs Enforcement, Secret Service, and FBI.

The second major governmental change occurred on November 25, 2002, with Congress approving the creation of the Department of Homeland Security. It marked the biggest government reorganization in American history. The department's mandate is to detect, prepare for, prevent, protect against, respond to, and recover from terrorist attacks within the United States. The Department of Homeland Security is an amalgamation of twenty-two separate government agencies merged into one department under one cabinet secretary designed to improve both communication and intelligence-sharing efforts across the entire spectrum of government.

To date, the effectiveness of Homeland Security has been mixed. To their well-deserved credit, our country hasn't suffered another foreign-led terrorist attack on our soil since 9/11. However, when it comes to the business of intelligence and counterterrorism, it isn't the plots you foil that matter most; it's the ones that you don't that do. One serious breach in security did occur on Christmas Day 2009, with the attempted downing of Northwest Flight 253 from Amsterdam to Detroit, Michigan. The would-be bomber, Umar Farouk Abdulmutallab, a radicalized Muslim and Nigerian citizen, successfully boarded a U.S.-bound airliner and attempted to ignite a plastic explosive with a syringe sewn into his underwear as the aircraft approached Detroit, Michigan. Had it not been for the quick action of Mr. Jasper Schuringa, a Dutch passenger who tackled the terrorist, the outcome could have been catastrophic. And another failed terrorist attempt which took place on May 1, 2010, when Faisal Shahzad, a Pakistani-born, naturalized American, attempted to set off a car bomb in New York City's Times Square.

These events were yet another wake-up call to our nation's leaders that, despite the great improvements we've made in our country's security since 9/11, more needs to be done. Our enemies are determined, capable, and continually devising new ways to strike us in the future.

As an American citizen, I support the incredible investment this country has made in the creation of NORTHCOM and the Department of Homeland Security, and I am certain that the leaders of these organizations will continually improve their programs and procedures and be tireless in their mission to keep America safe. I applaud all of them for their service. I also applaud the many other ordinary Americans who find the courage within themselves to react in times of crisis, often at their own peril, to ensure the survival of our great nation; the greatest generation this country has ever witnessed is the one carrying the burden we face today. May God bless you all, and may God continue to bless and protect the United States of America.

First Lieutenant Darling in Dhahran, Saudi Arabia, 1991

Captain Darling near his Cobra helicopter in Kuwait, 1993

Major Darling and Major Chip Rumsey before a Vice Presidential mission, 2000

*A visit from President Clinton's dog, Buddy,
inside Airlift Operations, 2000*

The collapse of The World Trade Center Towers after the terrorist attack using American Airlines Flight 11 and United Airlines Flight 175, September 11, 2001

The Pentagon burning after the terrorist attack using American Airlines Flight 77

An aerial view of the damage to the Pentagon caused by the impact of
American Airlines Flight 77

An aerial view of the carnage at Ground Zero, New York City

Cleanup operations continue day and night at Ground Zero

Firefighters and Urban Search and Rescue workers at Ground Zero

A Tribute to The World Trade Center Towers, September 2004

Major Darling in front of the VH-3D helicopter, aka Marine One

President Bush and Major Darling in the Oval Office, April 2002

I will not forget the wound to our country and those who inflicted it. I will not yield, I will not rest, I will not relent in waging this struggle for freedom and security for the American people.
—President George W. Bush
September 20, 2001

They have no moral inhibition on the slaughter of the innocent. If they could have murdered not 7,000 but 70,000, does anyone doubt they would have done so and rejoiced in it? There is no compromise possible with such people, no meeting of minds, no point of understanding with such terror. Just a choice: defeat it or be defeated by it. And defeat it we must!
—Tony Blair, British Prime Minister
Labor Party Conference

GLOSSARY OF TERMS

GOVERNMENT AGENCIES AND DEPARTMENTS

1. **CIA (Central Intelligence Agency):** Responsible for providing national-security intelligence to senior United States policymakers.
2. **DHS (Department of Homeland Security):** A department whose primary responsibilities include the protection of the territory of the United States from terrorist attacks and responding to natural disasters.
3. **DoD (Department of Defense):** The U.S. federal department charged with coordinating and supervising all agencies and functions of the government relating directly to national security and the United States armed forces.
4. **DIA (Defense Intelligence Agency):** A major producer and manager of military intelligence for the United States Department of Defense.
5. **FAA (Federal Aviation Administration):** An agency of the U.S. Department of Transportation with authority to regulate and oversee all aspects of civil aviation in the United States.
6. **FBI (Federal Bureau of Investigation):** An agency of the United States Department of Justice that serves as both a federal criminal investigative body and an internal intelligence agency.

7. **FEMA (Federal Emergency Management Agency):** An agency of the United States Department of Homeland Security responsible for coordinating the response to a disaster that has occurred in the United States and that overwhelms the resources of local and state authorities.

8. **ICE (Immigration and Customs Enforcement):** A federal law-enforcement agency under the United States Department of Homeland Security (DHS) responsible for identifying, investigating, and dismantling vulnerabilities regarding the nation's border, economic, transportation, and infrastructure security.

9. **NSA/CSS (The National Security Agency/Central Security Service):** A unit responsible for the collection and analysis of foreign communications and foreign signals intelligence, which involves cryptanalysis (code breaking).

10. **Senate Armed Services Committee:** A committee of the United States Senate empowered with legislative oversight of the nation's military and other matters pertaining to defense policy.

11. **TSA (Transportation Security Administration):** An agency created as part of the Aviation and Transportation Security Act passed by the U.S. Congress and signed into law by President George W. Bush on November 19, 2001. The TSA was originally organized in the U.S. Department of Transportation but was moved to the U.S. Department of Homeland Security on November 25, 2002.

AIRCRAFT

1. **AH-1W Cobra Helicopter:** Marine Corps attack helicopter that provides escort for assault helicopters and their embarked forces. The primary mission of the AH-1W aircraft is as an armed tactical helicopter capable of close air support and point target attack of threatening armor.

2. **Air Force One:** The official air-traffic-control call sign of any United States Air Force aircraft carrying the President of the United States. The presidential fleet consists of two specifically configured, highly customized Boeing 747-200B

series aircraft, Special Air Mission (SAM) 28000 and SAM 29000, with Air Force designation VC-25A.

3. **AWACS**: An airborne warning and control system aircraft. The Boeing E-3 Sentry, based on the Boeing 707, provides all-weather surveillance, command, control and communications to the United States, United Kingdom, France, Saudi Arabia, and NATO air-defense forces.

4. **B-2 Bomber** (also known as the Stealth Bomber): An American heavy bomber with low-observable stealth technology designed to penetrate dense anti-aircraft defenses and deploy both conventional and nuclear weapons.

5. **C-5 Galaxy:** A large, military transport aircraft designed to provide strategic heavy airlift over intercontinental distances.

6. **C-141 Starlifter:** A military strategic airlifter in service with the Air Mobility Command (AMC) of the U.S. Air Force.

7. **C-17 Globemaster:** A large military transport aircraft. It was developed for use by the U.S. Air Force. The C-17 is used for the rapid strategic airlift of troops and cargo to main operating bases or forward operating bases throughout the world.

8. **Crop duster:** An agricultural aircraft that has been built or converted for agricultural use—usually aerial application of pesticides (crop dusting) or fertilizer.

9. **E-4B**: An aircraft operated by the U.S. Air Force and specially built to serve as a survivable mobile command post for the National Command Authority, including the President of the United States, the Secretary of Defense, and other Presidential successors. The National Airborne Operations Center is a Boeing E-4 Advanced Airborne Command Post with the project name of Nightwatch.

10. **F-15 Eagle:** A twin-engine, all-weather tactical fighter designed to gain and maintain air superiority in aerial combat. Developed for the U.S. Air Force.

11. **F-16 Falcon:** A multirole jet fighter aircraft originally developed by General Dynamics for the U.S. Air Force.

12. **KC-10:** An air-to-air tanker aircraft in service with the U.S. Air Force.

13. **R-22:** A two-bladed, single-engine light utility helicopter manufactured by Robinson Helicopter

14. **VH-3D:** A twin-engine, all-weather helicopter flown by Marine Helicopter Squadron One (HMX-1) that supports the executive transport mission for the President of the United States. It has seating for sixteen passengers.

15. **VH-60N:** A twin-engine, all-weather helicopter flown by Marine Helicopter Squadron One (HMX-1) that supports the executive transport mission for the President of the United States. It has seating for ten passengers.

AIRPORTS AND AIR BASES

1. **Barksdale Air Force Base:** A base located three nautical miles east of the central business district of Bossier City in the state of Louisiana.

2. **John F. Kennedy Airport:** An international airport located in Queens County, New York, in southeastern New York City about twelve miles from lower Manhattan.

3. **Kelly Field Annex** (formerly Kelly Air Force Base): A U.S. Air Force facility located in San Antonio, Texas.

4. **LaGuardia Airport:** An airport located in Queens County on Long Island in the city of New York.

5. **Langley Air Force Base:** A base located three nautical miles north of the city of Hampton, Virginia. It is the home of the United States Air Force's First Fighter Wing (1 FW) and the 480th Intelligence Surveillance and Reconnaissance Wing (480 ISRW).

6. **Logan Airport:** An airport located in the East Boston neighborhood of Boston, Massachusetts. It is one of the twenty busiest airports in the United States, with more than twenty-six million passengers a year.

7. **Newark Airport:** An international airport within the city limits of both Newark and Elizabeth, New Jersey. It is about fifteen miles southwest of midtown Manhattan (New York City).

8. **Offutt Air Force Base:** A base near Omaha, Nebraska. It is the headquarters of the U.S. Strategic Command (USSTRATCOM).

9. **Otis Air National Guard Base:** An Air National Guard installation located within the Massachusetts Military Reservation (MMR), a military training facility located on the western portion of Cape Cod, in western Barnstable County, Massachusetts.

10. **Ramstein Air Force Base:** A U.S. Air Force base in the German state of Rheinland-Pfalz. It serves as headquarters for the United States Air Forces in Europe (USAFE) and is also a North Atlantic Treaty Organization (NATO) installation.

11. **Scott Air Force Base:** A base in St. Clair County, Illinois. The base serves as headquarters for the Air Mobility Command (AMC), the United States Transportation Command (USTRANSCOM), the Eighteenth Air Force (18 AF), the Air Force Global Logistics Support Center (AFGLSC), and the Air Force Network Integration Center.

12. **Stewart Air National Guard Base:** The home of the 105th Airlift Wing (105 AW), an Air Mobility Command (AMC). The former Stewart Air Force Base is also known as Newburgh-Stewart IAP and Stewart International Airport, while the military portion of this now-joint civil-military airport is known as Stewart Air National Guard Base.

13. **Whiteman Air Force Base:** The home of the 509th Bomb Wing, located 70 miles southeast of Kansas City, Missouri. The 509th Bomb Wing operates the B-2 Stealth Bomber.

14. **Yokota Air Force Base:** A U.S. installation located in Japan.

IMPORTANT PLACES

1. **Eisenhower Executive Office Building** (EEOB—formerly known as the Old Executive Office Building, or OEOB, and as the State, War, and Navy Building): An office building in Washington DC adjacent to the White House.

2. **National Military Command Center** (NMCC): A center located in the joint staff area of the Pentagon. The NMCC is responsible for generating Emergency Action Messages (EAMs) to launch control centers, nuclear submarines, recon aircraft, and battlefield commanders worldwide. The NMCC also provides joint staff with support and information relating to operational capabilities of the United States in the area of nuclear command and control, primarily missile warning systems of the Integrated Tactical Warning and Attack Assessment (ITW/AA) network.

3. **Naval Observatory:** One of the oldest scientific agencies in the United States. Its primary mission to produce Positioning, Navigation, and Timing for the U.S. Navy and the U.S. Department of Defense. Aside from its scientific mission, since 1974, the Observatory is also the official residence of the Vice President of the United States

4. **Pentagon:** The headquarters of the United States Department of Defense, located in Arlington, Virginia. As a symbol of the U.S. military, "the Pentagon" is often used metonymically to refer to the Department of Defense, rather than the building itself.

5. **President's Emergency Operations Center** (PEOC): A structure that lies beneath the White House. Originally constructed for President Franklin D. Roosevelt during World War II, it is presumed to be designed to withstand a nuclear blast. It is not the same place as the Situation Room, which is in the basement of the West Wing. However, it does possess several televisions, telephones, and a communications system to coordinate with other government entities during an emergency. The PEOC is manned around the clock by joint service military officers and NCOs.

6. **West Wing:** The building housing the official offices of the President of the United States. It is the part of the White House complex in which the Oval Office, the Cabinet Room, the Situation Room, and the Roosevelt Room are located. Besides serving as the day-to-day office of the President of the United States, the three floors of the West Wing include

offices for senior members of the Executive Office of the President of the United States and their support staff.

7. **White House Situation Room** (SitRoom): A five-thousand-square-foot conference room and intelligence-management center in the basement of the West Wing of the White House. It is run by the National Security Council staff for the use of the President of the United States and his advisors (including Homeland Security and the White House chief of staff) to monitor and deal with crises at home and abroad and to conduct secure communications with outside (often overseas) persons. The Situation Room is equipped with secure, advanced communications equipment for the President to maintain command and control of U.S. forces around the world.

UNIFIED COMBATANT COMMANDS

A **Unified Combatant Command** (UCC) is a joint military command that is composed of forces from two or more services, has a broad and continuing mission, and is organized either on a geographical basis (known as "area of responsibility," or AOR). All UCCs are commanded by either a four-star general or admiral and are considered joint commands with specific badges denoting their affiliation. UCCs (formerly known as COCOMs, a term now reserved exclusively for the authority they hold, which is also called "combatant command") are led by combatant commanders (CCDRs), formerly known as a regional Commander-in-Chief (CINC; pronounced "sink").

COMBATANT COMMANDS WITH REGIONAL RESPONSIBILITIES

- U.S. Africa Command (USAFRICOM)
- U.S. Central Command (USCENTCOM)
- U.S. European Command (USEUCOM)
- U.S. Pacific Command (USPACOM)
- U.S. Northern Command (USNORTHCOM)

- U.S. Southern Command (USSOUTHCOM)

COMBATANT COMMANDS WITH FUNCTIONAL RESPONSIBILITIES

- U.S. Joint Forces Command (USJFCOM)
- U.S. Special Operations Command (USSOCOM)
- U.S. Strategic Command (USSTRATCOM)
- U.S. Transportation Command (USTRANSCOM)

OTHER MILITARY TERMS

1. **AMRAAM:** The AIM-120 Advanced Medium-Range Air-to-Air Missile, or AMRAAM (pronounced am-ram), a modern beyond-visual-range (BVR), air-to-air missile (AAM) capable of all-weather day and night performance. It is also commonly known as the **Slammer** in USAF service. When an AMRAAM missile is being launched, NATO pilots use the brevity code **Fox Three.**

2. **Carrier Strike Group** (CSG): The term that replaces Carrier Battle Group in modern U.S. Navy carrier air operations. The CSG is centered on an aircraft carrier and its Carrier Air Wing. CSGs are an important part of the power-projection capability of the United States in that they provide the ability to strike quickly almost anywhere in the world.

3. **Continuity of Government** (COG): The principle of establishing defined procedures that allow a government to continue its essential operations in case of nuclear war or other catastrophic event.

4. **Continuity of Presidency** (COP): The principle of establishing defined procedures that allow the Executive Office of the President to continue its essential operations in case of nuclear war or other catastrophic event.

5. **Defense Condition** (DEFCON): A measure of the activation and readiness level of the U.S. armed forces. It describes progressive postures for use between the joint chiefs of staff and the commanders of unified commands. DEFCONs are matched to the situations of military severity.

Standard peacetime protocol is DEFCON 5, descending in increasingly severe situations. DEFCON 1 represents expectation of actual imminent attack and is not known to have ever been declared. During the Cold War, DEFCON 1 was feared, because it would most likely precede an all-out nuclear war.

6. **DEN (Domestic Events Network):** A nationwide, open phone line managed by the FAA to provide constant and clear communications for federal agencies with jurisdiction over the security of the United States.

7. **ESCAT:** Emergency Security Control of Air Traffic. This rule updates the national plan for security control of air traffic during air-defense emergencies.

8. **Forward Air Controller (FAC):** An officer who directs and controls close air-support missions and advises commanders on matters pertaining to air support.

9. **HUMVEE:** The High Mobility Multipurpose Wheeled Vehicle created for the U.S. military.

10. **ICBM:** Intercontinental Ballistic Missile. Long-range missile capable of carrying nuclear weapons.

11. **Marine One:** The official air-traffic-control call sign of any United States Marine Corps helicopter carrying the President of the United States.

12. **Marine Expeditionary Unit (MEU):** The smallest Marine Air-Ground Task Force in the United States Fleet Marine Force. Each MEU is an expeditionary quick-reaction force, deployed and ready for immediate response to any crisis.

13. **MedEvac:** Term used to describe aviation flights conducting medical evacuation.

14. **Military Aide to the President** (MilAide): A senior military officer (major or lieutenant colonel) assigned to the White House Military Office (WHMO) who accompanies the President and is responsible for carrying the "football," a black briefcase used by the President to authorize nuclear attack while away from fixed command centers, such as the White House Situation Room. The case functions as

a mobile hub in the strategic defense system of the United States.

15. **NEADS (North East Air Defense Sector):** A component of the North American Aerospace Defense Command (NORAD) located at the former Griffiss Air Force Base in Rome, New York. Responsible for providing detection and air defense for the entire eastern half of the United States.

16. **NORAD (North American Aerospace Defense Command):** A joint organization of Canada and the United States that provides aerospace warning, air sovereignty, and defense for the two countries. It was founded on May 12, 1958 (the effect of the Cold War), as a joint command between the governments of Canada and the United States.

17. **USNORTHCOM (U.S. Northern Command):** A unit established on October 1, 2002, in the aftermath of the September 11, 2001, attacks to protect the United States homeland and support local, state, and federal authorities.

18. **Prohibited Airspace:** Refers to an area of airspace in which flight of aircraft is not allowed, usually due to security concerns.

19. **Satellite Communications** (SATCOM): A communications satellite stationed in space for the purpose of telecommunications.

20. **Supersonic Flight:** A flight that exceeds the speed of sound **(Mach 1).** In dry air at 20 °C (68 °F), to travel at a supersonic speed is to go approximately 343 meters per second, (1,125 feet per second, 768 miles per hour, or 1,236 kilometers per hour).

NAVAL SHIPS

1. **USS George Washington (CVN 73):** The sixth ship in the *Nimitz* class of nuclear-powered super carriers and the fourth United States Navy ship to be named after George Washington, first President of the United States. It was built by Newport News Shipbuilding and was commissioned July 4, 1992.

2. **USS Intrepid (CV/CVA/CVS-11):** One of twenty-four *Essex*-class aircraft carriers built during World War II for the United States Navy. She is the fourth U.S. Navy ship to bear the name. Commissioned in August 1943, the *Intrepid* participated in several campaigns in the Pacific theater of operations, most notably the Battle of Leyte Gulf. Decommissioned shortly after the end of the war, she was modernized and recommissioned in the early 1950s as an attack carrier (CVA) and then became an antisubmarine carrier (CVS). In her second career, she served mainly in the Atlantic, but also participated in the Vietnam War. Her notable achievements include being the first U.S. aircraft carrier to launch aircraft with steam catapults and being the recovery ship for Mercury and a Gemini space mission. Because of her prominent role in battle, she was nicknamed "the Fighting I," while her time spent in dry dock for repairs earned her the nickname "the Dry I."

3. **USS John F. Kennedy (CV-67):** A decommissioned super carrier of the United States Navy. Nicknamed "Big John," it was named after the thirty-fifth President of the United States, John F. Kennedy. *Kennedy* was originally designated a CVA, or strictly an air-combat ship; however, the designation was changed to CV to denote that the ship was capable of antisubmarine warfare, making it an all-purpose carrier. After nearly forty years of service, the *Kennedy* was officially decommissioned on August 1, 2007.

ABOUT THE AUTHOR

**Robert J. Darling Lieutenant Colonel
United States Marine Corps (Ret.)**

Lieutenant Colonel Robert J. Darling retired from the U.S. Marine Corps on September 30, 2007, after serving his country for more than twenty years of honorable military service. He is currently a Vice President of business development for Zenetex, LLC, a premier IT service management and logistic support services company located in Herndon, Virginia.

As a public speaker, he has addressed numerous academic, government, military, and civic organizations to include the CIA, FBI, U.S. Marshals Service, Navy Space Warfare Center, U.S. Marine Corps, U.S. Air Force, Washington DC chapter of the Program Management Institute, Harvard University's John F. Kennedy School of Government, Iona College, Defense Language School, and the Military Officers' Association of America. He has also guest lectured on the subject of Crisis Leadership and Counterterrorism at the FBI National Academy in Quantico, Virginia. He currently lives in Stafford, Virginia, with his wife, Angela, and their two sons.

INDEX

Bold page numbers indicate photos.

A

AAM (air-to-air missile), 134

Abdulmutallab, Umar Farouk, 110–111

Adamcheck, Captain Wally (Irish), 19, 22–29, 102

adjutant, author as, 16–17

Advanced Medium-Range Air-to-Air Missiles (AMRAAM), 108, 134

AFGLSC (Air Force Global Logistics Support Center), 131

AH-1W Cobra helicopter, 128

aide, author as, 16–17

AIM-120 Advanced Medium-Range Air-to-Air Missile (AMRAAM), 134

Air Force
Air Force One. *See* Air Force One

aircraft used by, 129, 130. *See also specific aircraft*

bases, 130–131. *See also specific bases*

and control of all aircraft on 9/11, 59

Eighteenth Air Force (18 AF), 131

Glass Room, 81

and order to shoot down United Airlines Flight 93, 9/11, 54, 55

transportation of Bill Clinton, 9/11, 85–86

transportation of Cabinet members, 9/11, 80–85

as warriors in democracy's defense, post-9/11, 101

Air Force Global Logistics Support Center (AFGLSC), 131

Air Force Network Integration Center, 131

Air Force One
code word for, 61
described, 128
and job of Airlift Operations, 34
potential threat to, 60–62

141

presidential transportation, 35, 39, 69, 71, 72

protection of, 104

travel plan depictions of, 41

Air Mobility Command (AMC), 34, 35, 39, 41, 129, 131

Air Traffic Control System Command Center (ATCSCC), 52

airborne warning and control system aircraft (AWACS), 54, 129

aircraft, descriptions of, 128–130. *See also specific aircraft*

Airlift Operations
author's assignment to as liaison officer, 33

civilian deputy, Dennis Stump, 41

described, 33–34

director, Colonel Mike Irwin, 46

fulfillment of assignment, 9/11, 88

and news of first attack on World Trade Center, 9/11, 43

photo of office, **115**

reputation of, 70

shifting priorities of, 84

viewpoint of, regarding minivan for the President, 69

airports/air bases, 130–131

air-threat conferences, 9/11, 63, 72, 76

air-to-air missile (AAM), 134

Albaugh, Joe, 79

Alice Springs, Australia, Bill Clinton in, 9/11, 85

al-Qaeda, xix, 80

AMC (Air Mobility Command), 34, 35, 39, 41, 129, 131

American Airlines Flight 11, 9/11, 43, 102, 104, 106, 107, 108, 125

American Airlines Flight 77, 9/11, 92–93, 101, 105, 107, 108, 125

AMRAAM (Advanced Medium-Range Air-to-Air Missile), 108, 134

Andrews Air Force Base (Maryland), 35, 78, 84, 88, 91

Angel, as code for Air Force One, 61

area of responsibility (AOR), 133

Arlington, Virginia, 132

Army, as warriors in democracy's defense, post-9/11, 101

ATCSCC (Air Traffic Control System Command Center), 52

Atlanta, Georgia, 61

attire, work, 33, 37

Australia, Bill Clinton in, 9/11, 85

Aviation and Transportation Security Act (2001), 128

AWACS (airborne warning and control system aircraft), 54, 129

B

B-2 bomber (Stealth Bomber), 87, 129, 131

Bailey, Lieutenant Scott, 18

Baltimore, Maryland, 104, 107

Barksdale Air Force Base (Louisiana), 69, 71, 130

Barney (Bush family dog), 89

battle of Leyte Gulf, 137

beyond-visual-range (BVR), 134

"Big John" (USS *John F. Kennedy*), 137

bin Laden, Osama, 78

Blair, Tony, quote by, 126

Boeing 707, 129

Boeing 747-200B, 128–129

Boeing E-3 Sentry, 129

Boeing E-4 Advanced Airborne Command Post, 129

Bolton, Josh, 52

Bossier City, Louisiana, 130

Boston, Massachusetts, 130

Box. *See* Markin, Captain Tom (Box)

Bravo Company, Third Platoon, 12

Bravo uniform, 37

briefcase, black ("football"), 135–136

Buddy (President Clinton's dog), **115**

Bush, George W. *See also* President photo of, with author, **124**

quote by, 126

Bush, Laura, location of, on 9/11, 42

BVR (beyond-visual-range), 134

C

C-5 Galaxy, 129

C-17 Globemaster, 82, 84, 129

C-20 Learjet, 81, 82, 87

C-130, 41, 87

C-141 Starlifter, 85, 129

Cabinet members
line of succession to presidency, 70
reports from, 9/11, 79
transportation of, to DC, 9/11, 80–88, 91

Cabinet Room, 132

Cairns, Australia, Bill Clinton in, 9/11, 86

California, San Diego, Anthony Principi in, 9/11, 86

call signs, 16, 17–18, 19, 128

Canada, and NORAD, 136

cannons, use of, 19, 20, 22

Cantor Fitzgerald (financial services firm), 98

Cape Cod, Massachusetts, 131

car-bomb explosions, rumors of, 9/11, 68, 92

Carrier Battle Group, 134

Carrier Strike Group (CSG), 134

catastrophic events, procedures for, 57

CCDRs (combatant commanders), 133

CENTCOM. *See* USCENTCOM (U.S. Central Command)

Central Intelligence Agency (CIA), 76, 105, 127

CH-53E Sea Stallion, 32

Charlie uniform, 37

Cheney, Dick. *See also* Vice President (Dick Cheney)
author's support of, xx
background of, 53

in bunker, taking charge, 9/11,
51–53
comment on memory of United
Flight 93, 55
and Donald Rumsfeld,
attempting to contact, 9/11,
52–53
and Donald Rumsfeld,
conversation with , 9/11, 58
location of, on 9/11, 42
and Norman Mineta,
conversation with , 9/11, 59
order for firing solution of all
targets, 9/11, 62
order to engage all aircraft
inbound to Washington DC,
9/11, 62
order to ground civilian airliners,
9/11, 59
order to intercept "high-speed,
low-level" aircraft, 9/11, 71
order to intercept United Flight
93, 9/11, 53–55
order weapons free to engage,
9/11, 54
and President, phone calls to,
9/11, 56–57, 61
role of, on 9/11, xx–xxi
as warrior, 9/11, 53

Cheney, Lynn, 52

Chosin Reservoir (Korea), 13

CIA (Central Intelligence Agency),
76, 105, 127

CINC (regional Commander-in-
Chief), 133

CIRG (Critical Incident Response
Group). See FBI Critical Incident
Response Group (CIRG)

Clarke, Torie, 104, 105

Clinton, Bill
anecdote about, 32
dog of, **115**
transportation of, 9/11, 84–86,
87, 91

CNN, 43, 45, 56, 69, 75

Coast Guard, as warriors in
democracy's defense, post-9/11,
101

Cobra Court, 17

Cobra helicopter, 13, 16–19, 22–26,
28, **113**, 128

COCOM (combatant command),
133

Cold War, 135, 136

Combat Air Patrol, 104

combatant command (COCOM),
133

combatant commanders (CCDRs),
133

Commander in Chief, 69, 76, 77,
80. See also Bush, George W.;
President; President (George W.
Bush)

communications systems, overload
of, 9/11, 60

Continuity of Government (COG),
57, 67, 134

Continuity of Presidency (COP), 57,
67, 76, 134

Cooperider, Captain Stephen, 6–7

counterterrorism, 74, 110, 139

Cox, Major Andrew (Drew), 40

Crawford, Texas, 71

crisis-leadership skills, value of, 29

Critical Incident Response Group (CIRG). *See* FBI Critical Incident Response Group (CIRG)

crop duster
described, 129
not "bad guy" or "fast mover," 9/11, 71

Cruise, Tom, 15

CSG (Carrier Strike Group), 134

Cuban missile crisis, 63

CVAM (Department of Defense, Office of the Assistant Vice Chief of the Air Force, Special Assignment Air Mission Division), 34

D

Darling, Angela, 37, 43, 45–46, 92, 93, 94, 95–99, 102

Darling, Denis, 1, 6

Darling, Jeanette, xxiii

Darling, Matthew, 37, 92, 96

Darling, Michael, 37, 92, 96

Darling, Michael (father), 1

Darling, Neil, 1

Darling, Robert (Bob)
as Captain, **113**
as First Lieutenant, **112**
as Major, **114, 115, 123, 124**

Darling, Sean, 1, 44

death toll
from 9/11 attacks, 78, 98
on service members, post-9/11, 99

DEFCON 1, 135

DEFCON 2, 63, 64

DEFCON 3, 63, 64, 71

DEFCON 5, 135

DEFCONs (Defense Conditions), 134

Defense Intelligence Agency (DIA), 127

DEN (Domestic Events Network), 110, 135

Department of Defense (DoD), 33–34, 45, 52, 58, 109, 110, 127, 132

Department of Homeland Security (DHS), 110, 111, 127, 128, 133

Deputy National Security Advisor (Stephen Hadley), 57. *See also* Hadley, Stephen

Desert Shield, 29

Desert Storm, 29

Dhahran, Saudi Arabia, 16, 112

DHS (Department of Homeland Security), 110, 111, 127, 128, 133

DIA (Defense Intelligence Agency), 127

DiRita, Larry, 104, 105

divine intervention, possibility of, 29

DoD (Department of Defense), 33–34, 45, 52, 58, 109, 110, 127, 132

Domestic Events Network (DEN), 110, 135

doomsday planes, 93

Dover Air Force Base, 87

"the Dry I" (USS *Intrepid*), 137

E

E-4B aircraft, 93, 129

Eager Mace, 15

EAMs (Emergency Action Messages), 132

Eberhart, General Ralph, 107

Eighteenth Air Force (18 AF), 131

Eisenhower Executive Office Building (EEOB), 40, 45, 46, 50, 131

Elizabeth, New Jersey, 130

Ellipse (park), 40, 47

Emergency Action Messages (EAMs), 132

Emergency Security Control of Air Traffic (ESCAT), 73, 135

Emma E. Booker Elementary School, 35

England, Mildenhall, Alan Greenspan in, 9/11, 81

ESC (Executive Support Center) (Pentagon), 105

ESCAT (Emergency Security Control of Air Traffic), 73, 135

Essex class (Navy ships), 137

EUCOM. *See* USEUCOM (U.S. European Command)

evacuations, of buildings, on 9/11, 46, 47, 68

Evans, Donald, 79

Everett, Matthew, 104

Executive Office of the President of the United States

and Continuity of Presidency (COP), 134

location of, 132–133

Executive Support Center (ESC) (Pentagon), 105

F

F-15 aircraft, 53, 54, 55, 103, 106, 129

F-16 aircraft, 71, 89, 104, 106, 107, 108, 129

FAA (Federal Aviation Administration), 52, 59, 104, 106, 109, 110, 127, 135

FAC (forward air controller), 19, 135

fatalities
9/11, xix, 78, 102
post-9/11, of service members, 101

FBI (Federal Bureau of Investigation), 73, 74, 75, 76. *See also* FBI Critical Incident Response Group (CIRG); FBI Hostage Rescue Team

FBI Critical Incident Response Group (CIRG), 73–74, 75, 88, 110, 127

FBI Field Office, San Francisco, 75

FBI Hostage Rescue Team, 74

Federal Aviation Administration (FAA), 52, 59, 104, 106, 109, 110, 127, 135

Federal Bureau of Investigation (FBI), 73, 74, 75, 76. *See also* FBI Critical Incident Response Group (CIRG); FBI Hostage Rescue Team

Federal Reserve Chairman (Alan Greenspan), 80, 81, 91. *See also* Greenspan, Alan

FEMA (Federal Emergency Management Agency), 45, 56, 79, 128

"the Fighting I" (USS *Intrepid*), 137

First Fighter Wing (1 FW), 130

First Lady
location of, on 9/11, 42
middle-of-night trip to bunker, 9/12, 89
transportation of, 35, 41

first responders, 9/11, 45, 53, 98, 102, 109

Fish, call sign for forward air controller (FAC), 19, 20, 21, 22

509th Bomb Wing, 131

flares, use of, 21, 22

Florida
Pensacola, 29
Sarasota, 35, 39, 42

"football" (black briefcase), 135–136

forward air controller (FAC), 19, 135

480th Intelligence Surveillance and Reconnaissance Wing (480 ISRW), 130

Fox Three, brevity code for AMRAAM missile launch, 134

France, and AWACS (airborne warning and control system aircraft), 129

G

Gemini space mission, 137

Georgia, Atlanta, 61

Germany, Ramstein Air Force Base, 81, 131

Giuliani, Rudy, 56

Glass Room, 81

glossary, 127–137

Gore, Al, 32–33

government agencies/departments, 127–128. *See also* specific agencies/departments

Graceland, 32

Greenspan, Alan, 82, 91. *See also* Federal Reserve Chairman (Alan Greenspan)

Griffis Air Base (New York), 136

Ground Zero, 98, **119, 120, 121**

grounding of general aviation and commercial aircraft, 9/11, 59, 73

Guam
Bill Clinton in, 9/11, 85, 86
George W. Bush trip to, 41

Gulf War, first, 16

H

Hadley, Stephen, 52, 61

Hagin, Joe, 73, 80, 91. *See also* White House Deputy Chief of Staff (Joe Hagin)

Hampton, Virginia, 130

helicopter flying
aircraft used, 17, 128, 130, 135. *See also* Cobra helicopter

described, 23
landing on South Lawn, 31, 35, 78

Herndon, Virginia, 52

high-occupancy vehicles (HOVs), 38

HMX-1 (Marine Helicopter Squadron One), 31, 32, 33, 130

Hostage Rescue Team, 74

HOVs (high-occupancy vehicles), 38

Huey helicopter, 17

Hughes, Karen, 77

Humvee
described, 135
as presidential vehicle, 70

Hussein, Saddam, 16

I

Ia Drang (Vietnam), 13

ICBM (Intercontinental Ballistic Missile), 66, 135

Illinois
Scott Air Force Base, 34, 81, 131
St. Clair County, 81, 131

Immigration and Customs Enforcement (ICE), 110, 128

Integrated Tactical Warning and Attack Assessment (ITW/AA), 132

intelligence, business of, 76, 78, 110. *See also* CIA (Central Intelligence Agency); DIA (Defense Intelligence Agency); FBI (Federal Bureau of Investigation); NSA/CSS (The National Security Agency/Central Security Service)

interception, possibility of, 9/11, American Airlines Flight 77, 107

interception missions, 9/11
American Airlines Flight 11, 104
crop duster, 71
United Airlines Flight 93, 54

Intercontinental Ballistic Missile (ICBM), 66, 135

Iona College, 2, 13, 98, 102

Iow Jima, 13

Iraqi army, 16

Irish (Captain Wally Adamcheck). *See* Adamcheck, Captain Wally (Irish)

Irwin, Colonel Mike, 46, 47, 73, 85

ITW/AA (Integrated Tactical Warning and Attack Assessment), 132

Iwakuni, Japan, Paul O'Neill in, 9/11, 84

J

Japan, Paul O'Neill in, 9/11, 85

John F. Kennedy Airport (New York), 130

K

Kansas City, Missouri, 131

KC-10 tanker, 82, 86, 130

Kelly Air Force Base (Texas), 71, 130

Kelly Field Annex (Texas), 130

Kennedy, John F., 137

Kid. *See* Manny, First Lieutenant Ken (Kid)

Korea, Chosin Reservoir, 13

Kuwait, 15, 18, **113**

Kuwait International Airport, 23, 24, 25

L

Lafayette Park, 47

LaGuardia Airport (New York), 130

Langley Air Force Base (Virginia), 104, 106, 107, 130

language issues, with foreign airport personnel, 25–26

The Late Show with David Letterman (TV program), 32–33

Leadership Reaction Course (LRC), 10–12

Leyte Gulf, battle of, 137

Libby, Scooter, 52

Lima, Peru, Colin Powell in, 9/11, 70

Lincoln, Abraham, 78

Logan Airport (Boston), 106, 130

Long Island, New York, 54, 106, 130

Louisiana
  Bossier City, 130
  Shreveport, 69

low-altitude alarm, 21

LRC (Leadership Reaction Course), 10–12

luck, possibility of, 29

M

Madison, James, 78

Manhattan, New York, 2, 6, 13, 64, 95, 96, 106, 130

Manny, First Lieutenant Ken (Kid), 19–22, 24, 26–29, 102

Marine Air-Ground Task Force, 135

Marine Corps
  Officer Candidate School (OCS), 5, 12, 13
  Platoon Leader Class (PLC), 5–6, 7, 8
  as warriors in democracy's defense, 101

Marine Expeditionary Unit (MEU), 15, 135

Marine Helicopter Squadron One (HMX-1), 31, 32, 33, 130

Marine One, 34, 35, 42, 78, **123**, 135

Marine Two, 32

Markin, Captain Tom (Box), 19–29, 102

Marr, Colonel Robert, 109

Maryland, Baltimore, 104, 107

Massachusetts
  Boston, 130
  Cape Cod, 131
  Logan Airport (Boston), 106, 130
  Otis Air Force Base, 106
  Otis Air National Guard Base, 53, 131

Massachusetts Military Reservation (MMR), 131

Maverick, as call sign, 16

McGyver, John, 5, 6, 13, 102

McMahon, Technical Sergeant Mike, 40, 44, 45

MedEvac
described, 135
helicopter incident, 9/11, 59, 92, 108

Mercury space mission, 137

MEU (Marine Expeditionary Unit), 135

Mildenhall, England, Alan Greenspan in, 9/11, 81

Military Aide to the President (MilAide), 135

military terms, 133–134

Mineta, Norman, 57, 59, 79

minivan, as presidential vehicle, 69–70

Miramar Naval Air Station, Anthony Principi in, 87

Missouri
Kansas City, 131
Whiteman Air Force Base, 87, 131

Mitchell, Lieutenant Pete (fictional character), 15

MMR (Massachusetts Military Reservation), 131

mole, possibility of, on Air Force One, 9/11, 60–61

Morenic, Colonel, 83

Morris, Maureen, xxiii

N

National Airborne Operations Center, 93, 129

National Capitol Police, 110

National Cemetery, 12

National Command Authority (NCA)
aircraft used by, 129
flaws in, 109
ineffectiveness of, on 9/11, xx, 109
location of, on 9/11, 103–105
logistical and communications center, 52
National Airborne Operations Center, 93
vital role of, 53

National Military Command Center (NMCC). *See* NMCC (National Military Command Center)

National Security Advisor, 63, 67, 68, 103. *See also* Rice, Condoleezza

National Security Agency (NSA), 76

National Security Agency/Central Security Service (NSA/CSS), 128

National Security Council, 72, 133

NATO (North Atlantic Treaty Organization), 129, 131

Naval Observatory, 132

Naval Reserve Officer Training Course (NROTC), 5

naval ships, 136–137. *See also specific ships*

Navy

and Airlift Operations, 34
Carrier Strike Group (CSG), 134
deployment of battle group, 9/11,
71, 72
ships, 136–137
and tracking of targets, 9/11, 62
as warriors in democracy's
defense, post-9/11, 101

NCA (National Command
Authority). *See* National
Command Authority (NCA)

NEADS (North East Air Defense
Sector), 106, 107, 109, 136

Nebraska, Offut Air Force Base, 71,
72, 93, 131

New Jersey
Elizabeth, 130
Newark, 130

New Rochelle, New York, 2

New York
Griffis Air Base, 136
John F. Kennedy Airport, 130
LaGuardia Airport, 130
Long Island, 54, 106, 130
Manhattan, 2, 6, 13, 95, 96, 106,
130
New Rochelle, 2
New York City. *See* New York
City, 9/11
Newburgh, 1, 44, 86, 131
Rome, 136
Stewart Air Force Base, 131
Stewart Air National Guard Base,
86, 91, 131
Stewart International Airport, 131

New York City, 9/11
civilian death toll, 78, 102
disfigurement of skyline, 102

firefighters and police officers
missing and presumed dead, 78,
102
first responders, 45, 102. *See also*
first responders
news of first attack on, 43
news of full-blown terrorist attack
on, 44
support for, 56, 79, 87, 88

Newark, New Jersey, 130

Newark Airport (New Jersey), 130

Newburgh, New York, 1, 44, 86

Newburgh-Stewart IAP, 131

Newport News Shipbuilding, 136

Nighthawks (Marine Helicopter
Squadron One) (HMX-1), 29

night-vision goggles (NVGs), 18, 19,
20, 21, 22

Nightwatch, 129

Nimitz class (Navy ships), 136

9/11 attacks, 43–45. *See also*
Pentagon, attack on, 9/11; World
Trade Center

9/11 Commission, xx, xxi

NMCC (National Military
Command Center), 52, 53, 54,
55, 61, 62, 70, 71, 81, 105, 106,
108, 132

NORAD (North American
Aerospace Defense Command),
59, 60, 62, 69, 73, 74, 75, 80, 81,
107, 110, 136

Norfolk, Virginia, 71

North American Aerospace Defense Command (NORAD). *See* NORAD (North American Aerospace Defense Command)

North Atlantic Treaty Organization (NATO), 129, 131

North East Air Defense Sector (NEADS). *See* NEADS (North East Air Defense Sector)

North Tower. *See* World Trade Center, North Tower, 9/11

NORTHCOM (U.S. Northern Command). *See* USNORTHCOM (U.S. Northern Command)

Northwest Airlines Flight 253, 12/25/09, 110–111

NROTC (Naval Reserve Officer Training Course), 5

NSA (National Security Agency), 76

NSA/CSS (The National Security Agency/Central Security Service), 128

Nuclear Risk Reduction Center, 66

NVGs (night-vision goggles), 18, 19, 20, 21, 22

O

OCS (Marine Corps Officer Candidate School), 5, 12, 13, 102

"off cold," 20, 21

Offutt Air Force Base (Nebraska), 71, 72, 93, 131

Old Executive Office Building (OEOB), 131

105th Airlift Wing (105 AW), 131

O'Neill, Paul, 80, 83. *See also* Secretary of the Treasury (Paul O'Neill)

Online Journal, 104

Otis Air Force Base (Massachusetts), 106

Otis Air National Guard Base (Massachusetts), 53, 131

Oval Office, 80, **124**, 132

P

PACOM. *See* USPACOM (U.S. Pacific Command)

PDB (president's daily briefing book), 76

Pennsylvania
Pittsburgh, 51, 52, 53, 54, 108
Shanksville, 74, 108

Pensacola, Florida, 29

Pentagon
attack on, 9/11, 45, 47, 107–108, **117**
damage to, 9/11, 56, 92–93, **118**
dead and wounded at, 9/11, 78
described, 132
memorial at, 101

PEOC (President's Emergency Operations Center), xx, 47, 50–51, 54, 55, 56, 78, 132

Persian Gulf, 15, 18

Peru, Lima, Colin Powell in, 9/11, 70

Phoenix missions
Banner, 35
Copper, 35
Silver, 35

Pittsburgh, Pennsylvania, 51, 52, 53, 54, 108

PLC (Marine Corps Platoon Leader Class), 5–6, 7, 8

POTUS (President of the United States), 42

Powell, Colin, 70, 79

presidency, line of succession to, 67, 71

President
daily briefing book (PDB), 76
day-to-day office of, 132
military aide to, 135
and National Command Authority, 103
official offices of, 132
POTUS, acronym for, 42
transportation of, 31, 33–34, 35, 41

President (George W. Bush). *See also* Bush, George W.
address to the nation 9/11, 77
air-threat conference, convening of, 9/11, 63, 72, 76
at Barksdale Air Force Base, 9/11, 69, 71
Cabinet members and Vice President, reports from, 9/11, 79
and Dick Cheney, phone calls, 9/11, 56–57, 61
middle-of-night trip to bunker, 9/12, 89
potential threat to, 9/11, 61
return to the White House, 9/11, 78
in Sarasota, Florida, 9/11, 35, 39
speech-writing process, 77
at STRATCOM, 9/11, 76

President of the United States (POTUS), 42

President's Emergency Operations Center (PEOC). *See* PEOC (President's Emergency Operations Center)

Princiotta, Vincent, 88

Principi, Anthony, transportation of, post-9/11, 80, 86–88

priorities, shifting of, 84

prohibited airspace, defined, 136

Putin, Vladimir, phone call to Situation Room, 9/11, 65–66

Q

Quantico, Virginia, 5, 8, 12, 29, 102

R

R-22 helicopter, 130

racetrack attack pattern, 21

Ramstein Air Force Base (Germany), 81, 131

Reagan National Airport (Washington DC), 88

regional Commander-in-Chief (CINC), 133

Renuart, General Victor, 110

Rice, Condoleezza
airliners, accounting for, 9/11, 69
and Angel, report of as next target, 9/11, 60–61
author's support of, xx
in bunker, 9/11, 52
and DEFCON status, reaction to upgrade, 9/11, 63

and President, counseling not to return, 9/11, 76

and President, meeting of Marine One upon return, 9/11, 78

and President, preparation for return of, 9/11, 77

and President, report to, 9/11, 79

and rumor of car-bomb explosions, 9/11, 60

Speaker of the House, search for, 9/11, 67–68

and Vladimir Putin, phone call with, 9/11, 65–66

Robinson Helicopter, 130

Rome, New York, 136

Roosevelt, Franklin D., 132

Roosevelt Room, 132

Rules of Engagement (ROE), 107

rumors, on 9/11, 60, 68, 92

Rumsey, Major Chip, 33, **114**

Rumsfeld, Donald. *See also* Secretary of Defense (Donald Rumsfeld)
location of, on 9/11, 103–105, 108–109
recommendation to raise to DEFCON 3, 9/11, 63
Vice President attempting to contact, 9/11, 52, 53
Vice President connecting with, 9/11, 58

Russian response, 9/11, 65–66

S

SAAMs (Special-Assignment Air Missions), 41

San Antonio, Texas, 71, 130

San Diego, California, Anthony Principi in, 9/11, 86

sand dunes, 18

Santayana, George, 102

Sarasota, Florida, 35, 39, 42

satellite communications (SATCOM), defined, 136

Saudi Arabia, 16, 112, 129

Schuringa, Jasper, 111

Scott Air Force Base (Illinois), 34, 81, 131

Secret Service, 34, 35, 41, 42, 47, 57, 61, 76, 77, 84, 85, 89, 110

Secretary of Defense (Donald Rumsfeld). *See also* Rumsfeld, Donald
on air-threat conference, 9/11, 73
as authority regarding Rules of Engagement (ROE), 107
and line of succession to the presidency, 70
location of, on 9/11, 103–105
and National Command Authority, 103
and President, contact with, 9/11, xx
and President and Vice President, discussion with, 9/11, 72
recommendation to raise to DEFCON 3, 9/11, 63
and Vice President attempting to contact, 9/11, 52–53, 58

Secretary of State (Colin Powell). *See* Powell, Colin

Secretary of the Treasurer (Donald Evans), 79

Secretary of the Treasury (Paul O'Neill), 79, 80, 83

Secretary of Transportation (Norman Mineta), 79. *See also* Mineta, Norman

Secretary of Veterans Affairs (Anthony Principi), 80, 86. *See also* Principi, Anthony

security
breaches of, post-9/11, 110–111
improvements in, post-9/11, 109

Senate Armed Services Committee, 128

September 11, 2001, chronology of attacks, 43–45. *See also* 9/11 Commission; Pentagon, attack on, 9/11; World Trade Center

service members
dead, post-9/11, 101
wounded, post-9/11, 101

Shahzad, Faisal, 111

Shanksville, Pennsylvania, 74, 108

Sharpy, Major Tom, 51, 57, 61, 77

shoot-down orders, 9/11
of so-called targets, 62
of United Airlines Flight 93, 53, 108

Shreveport, Louisiana, 69

Shyster, as call sign, 16, 18

Sikorsky VH-3D, 31, 32. *See also* VH-3D helicopter

Sikorsky VH-60N, 31, 32. *See also* VH-60N helicopter

Situation Room, 9/11, 50, 51, 52, 56, 57, 132, 133

skids, on Cobra helicopter, 24, 25, 26

Slammer (AMRAAM), 134

slugging, 38

Somalia, 15, 29

South Lawn, of the White House, 31, 35, 78

South Tower. *See* World Trade Center, South Tower, 9/11

SOUTHCOM. *See* USSOUTHCOM (U.S. Southern Command)

Speaker of the House
attempt to locate, 9/11, 67–68
and line of succession to the presidency, 67

Special Air Mission (SAM) 28000, 129

Special Air Mission (SAM) 29000, 129

Special-Assignment Air Mission Flight 8811, 75, 88–89

Special-Assignment Air Missions (SAAMs), 41

speech-writing process, 77

St. Clair County, Illinois, 81, 131

Stafford, Virginia, 37

State, War, and Navy Building, 131

State Department, 60, 66, 92

Stealth Bomber (B-2 bomber), 87, 129, 131

Stewart Air Force Base (New York), 131

Stewart Air National Guard Base (New York), 86, 91, 131

Stewart International Airport, 131

STRATCOM. *See* USSTRATCOM (U.S. Strategic Command)

Stump, Dennis, 41, 42, 44

Sullivan, Tim, 5, 6, 13, 102

supersonic flights, defined, 136

T

Taliban, 80

Tank, 50. *See also* Situation Room

terrorists/terrorism, 79, 80, 97, 101, 110

Texas
Crawford, 71
Kelly Air Force Base, 71, 130
Kelly Field Annex, 130
San Antonio, 71, 130

Tillman, Colonel Mark, 61

Times Square, 111

Top Gun (movie), 15

transportation, post-9/11, 79

Transportation Security Administration (TSA), 110, 128

Trauma One, 34

Twenty-fourth Marine Expeditionary Unit (MEU), 15

Twin Towers, 9/11, 47, 64, 96, 99. *See also* World Trade Center

U

Udairi Range, 18

Unified Combatant Commands (UCCs), 64, 133

uniforms, 37

United Airlines
and FBI Hostage Rescue Team, 74–75, 76
Flight 93. See United Airlines Flight 93, 9/11

United Airlines Flight 93, 9/11, 51, 53, 55, 74, 92, 97, 98, 101, 103, 108, 109, 125

United Airlines Flight 175, 9/11, 102, 106, 125

United Kingdom, and AWACS (airborne warning and control system aircraft), 129

United States Air Forces in Europe (USAFE), 131

U.S. Africa Command (USAFRICOM), 133

U.S. Airways flight, 9/11, potential hostage situation on board, 72

U.S. Central Command (USCENTCOM), 64, 133

U.S. Code of Federal Regulations, 70, 73, 85

U.S. Department of Defense (DoD). *See* Department of Defense (DoD)

U.S. Department of Homeland Security. *See* Department of Homeland Security (DHS)

U.S. Department of Justice, 127

U.S. Department of Transportation, 127, 128

U.S. European Command (USEUCOM), 64, 133

U.S. Joint Forces Command (USJFCOM), 134

U.S. Northern Command (USNORTHCOM), 109–110, 111, 133, 136

U.S. Pacific Command (USPACOM), 64, 133

U.S. Southern Command (USSOUTHCOM), 64, 134

U.S. Special Operations Command (USSOCOM), 134

U.S. Strategic Command (USSTRATCOM), 59, 64, 76, 131, 134

U.S. Transportation Command (USTRANSCOM), 131, 134

USAFRICOM (U.S. Africa Command), 133

USCENTCOM (U.S. Central Command), 64, 133

USEUCOM (U.S. European Command), 64, 133

USJFCOM (U.S. Joint Forces Command), 134

USNORTHCOM (U.S. Northern Command), 109–110, 111, 133, 136

USPACOM (U.S. Pacific Command), 64, 133

USS *George Washington*, 71, 136

USS *Intrepid*, 13, 99, 137

USS *John F. Kennedy*, 71, 137

USSOCOM (U.S. Special Operations Command), 134

USSOUTHCOM (U.S. Southern Command), 64, 134

USSTRATCOM (U.S. Strategic Command), 59, 64, 76, 131, 134

USTRANSCOM (U.S. Transportation Command), 131, 134

V

VC-25A, 129

vertical-climb situation, 22

Veterans Administration, 86

VH-3D helicopter, 31, 32, **123**, 130

VH-60N helicopter, 31, 32, 130

Vice President
and line of succession to the presidency, 67, 70
official residence of, 132
transportation of, 31, 33–34, 35, 41

Vice President (Dick Cheney). *See also* Cheney, Dick
accounting for airliners, 9/11, 69
air-threat conference, 9/11, 63, 73
call for all "actionable intelligence," 9/11, 76
and Donald Rumsfeld, contact with, 9/11, 58
location of, on 9/11, 42
and Norman Mineta, conversation with, 9/11, 59
order for fighter escorts for Air Force One, 9/11, 61
order to ground all civilian airliners, 9/11, 59
order to raise national defense posture to DEFCON 3, 9/11, 63

order to shoot down United
Airlines Flight 93, 9/11, 103
and President, phone calls to,
9/11, 56–57, 61
and President, report to, 9/11, 79
review of U.S. Airways airliner
bound from Madrid, 72
tough decisions by, 9/11, xx,
103–104, 109

Vietnam War, 137

Virginia

Hampton, 130

Herndon, 52

Langley Air Force Base, 104, 106,
107, 130

Norfolk, 71

Quantico, 5, 8, 12, 29, 102

Stafford, Virginia, 37

W

War Room, 50. *See also* Situation
Room

Washington, George, 31

Washington DC
and American Airlines Flight 11,
9/11, 106
and American Airlines Flight 77,
9/11, 93, 107, 108, 109
historical attacks on, 78
order to engage all aircraft
inbound to, 9/11, 62
Reagan National Airport, 88
and United Flight 93, 9/11, 51,
52, 53, 54, 108

weapons free to engage, 54

West Wing, 47, 51, 132, 133

WHCA (White House
Communications Agency), 34

White House
appearance of attack on, 57–59
evacuation of, 46

White House Airlift Operations, 33.
See also Airlift Operations

White House bunker, 43

White House Chief of Staff, 133

White House Communications
Agency (WHCA), 34

White House Deputy Chief of Staff
(Joe Hagin), 73, 75, 80, 91

White House Military Office
(WHMO), 33, 35, 51, 73, 135

White House military presence
current status, 31
origins of, 31

White House Situation Room
(SitRoom), 133

White House Special-Assignment
Air Mission, 74

Whiteman Air Force Base
(Missouri), 87, 131

WHMO (White House Military
Office), 33, 35, 51, 73, 135

wing stubs, on Cobra helicopter, 25,
26, 28

World Trade Center
collapse of, 9/11, **116**
death toll at, 9/11, 102
news of first attack on, 9/11, 43
North Tower, 9/11, 43, 98, 106
South Tower, 9/11, 44, 56, 106
tribute to, **122**

Twin Towers. *See* Twin Towers

World War II, 132

Y
Yokota Air Force Base (Japan), 84,
131

Z
Zurich, Switzerland, Alan
Greenspan in, 9/11, 80, 81